Separation of Church and State

MERCER
UNIVERSITY PRESS

Endowed by
TOM WATSON BROWN
and
THE WATSON-BROWN FOUNDATION, INC.

Separation *of* Church *and* State

Founding Principle of Religious Liberty

FRANK LAMBERT

Mercer University Press
Macon, Georgia

MUP/ H884

Published by Mercer University Press, Macon, Georgia 31207
© 2014 Mercer University Press
1400 Coleman Avenue
Macon, Georgia 31207

9 8 7 6 5 4 3 2 1

Books published by Mercer University Press are printed on
acid-free paper that meets the requirements of the American
National Standard for Information Sciences—Permanence of
Paper for Printed Library Materials.

Library of Congress Cataloging-in-Publication Data

Lambert, Frank, 1943-
  Separation of church and state : founding principle of religious liberty /
Frank Lambert.
     pages cm.
  Includes bibliographical references and index.
  ISBN-13: 978-0-88146-477-1 (hardback : alkaline paper)
  ISBN-10: 0-88146-477-5 (hardback : alkaline paper)
1. Church and state--United States--History. 2. Christianity and politics-
-United States--History. 3. Religious right--United States--History.
4. Right and left (Political science) 5. Christians--Political activity. I.
Title.
  BR516.L295 2014
  322'.10973--dc23
                                                        2014000356

Contents

For Walter and Kay Shurden

Acknowledgments

Mercer University professors Walter and Kay Shurden made this book possible—literally. In April 2012 I delivered the Walter B. and Kay W. Shurden Lectures on Religious Liberty and Separation of Church and State at Mercer, an annual program sponsored by the Baptist Joint Committee and endowed by the Shurdens.

In 1972 I first met Buddy, as he is known to his friends, when I took his course on Baptist History at the Southern Baptist Theological Seminary in Louisville, Kentucky. A visiting professor from Carson-Newman University, Buddy both challenged and inspired his students to think deeply about such issues as religious liberty and church-state relations and to seek their roots through careful analysis of primary source documents. I was further inspired by reading his book, *Not a Silent People, Controversies That Have Shaped Southern Baptists* (1972), especially his discussion of questions about religious freedom. Little did I know at the time that it would be that idea and that book that would influence my own research agenda.

I am also indebted to the fine staff of the Baptist Joint Committee who organized the lectures at Mercer. In particular, I wish to thank Executive Director J. Brent Walker and General Counsel Hollyn Hollman for their gracious assistance and encouragement.

I owe much thanks to Brigitta van Rheinberg, Editor-in-Chief and Executive Editor of Princeton University Press, for granting permission to draw upon the following works that I published with Princeton: *"Pedlar in Divinity:" George Whitefield and the Transatlantic Revivals, 1737–1770* (1994); *Inventing the "Great Awakening"* (1999); *The Founding Fathers and the Place of Religion in America* (2003); and *Religion in American Politics: a Short History* (2008). Having worked closely with Brigitta on two of those books, I am aware of the importance of an acquisitions editor in shaping a project from initial conception to final publication. In this book, I have the privilege of working with Marc A. Jolley, Director of Mercer University Press.

Finally, I owe the most to my wife, Beth, who suggested that I publish the lectures for a general audience. As always, she is what every author needs at home: an honest and fair critic and a loyal ally.

Separation *of* Church *and* State

Introduction

For Jasper Adams the separation of church and state was incomprehensible. He judged the argument "that Christianity has no connexion with our civil Constitutions of government...[to be] one of those which admit of being tested by the absurd and dangerous consequences to which they lead." As he looked about him in 1833, the Episcopal priest and president of Charleston College lamented such "dangerous consequences" as the recent law making the Sabbath another day for commerce rather than setting it aside as a holy day of worship. In what he called an "inductive examination" of the United States Constitution, Adams argued that although the Constitution "contains but slight references of a religious kind," the "people of the United States profess themselves to be a Christian nation." He arrived at that conclusion from the date affixed to the document: "in the Year of our Lord seventeen hundred and Eighty seven." Rather than regarding the wording of the date as a convention widely used on all sorts of papers, including those associated with commerce, Adams construed it to be a profession of faith. He claimed that "Lord" means the "Lord Jesus Christ" and that "our" refers to "We the People," and thus he read the Constitution as the people confessing themselves to be constituted as a Christian nation.[1]

---

[1] Adams wrote his sermon in 1832 and it was published in 1833. See Jasper Adams, *The Relation of Christianity to Civil Government in the United States,* 2nd ed. (Charleston: A.E. Miller, 1833).

Adams based his case on a dating convention used throughout the Western Hemisphere by Catholics, Protestants, and Infidels. Devised by a Scythian monk, Dionysius Exiguus, in the midst of a sixth-century dispute within Christendom over the date for Easter, it became the accepted way of reckoning dates in the West. Why did Adams rest his argument on such a weak reed? That was all the Constitution gave him. Although the Preamble lists six purposes for forming the new republic, establishing a Christian or religious state is not one of them. Surely if their intention was to create a Christian state, the framers would have stated it clearly and boldly, perhaps, "In order to create a Christian State...." If their model had been the Christian states erected by Puritans in seventeenth-century Connecticut and Massachusetts Bay, they would have made explicit reference to Jesus Christ and would have made the advancement of the Gospel the major aim of the Constitution. But, to the dismay of many, the delegates made no reference to God or divine inspiration. As Yale President Timothy Dwight put it twenty-five years later, "We formed our Constitution without any acknowledgement of God; without any recognition of his mercies to us, as a people, of his government, of even his existence. The [Constitutional] Convention, by which it was formed, never asked, even once, his direction, or his blessing upon his labours. Thus we commenced our national existence under the present system, without God."[2]

Adams blamed secularists for reducing Christian influence in public affairs. He charged the Deists, Benjamin Franklin and Thomas Jefferson, with starting the process of

---

[2] Cited in Harry Stout, "Rhetoric and Reality in the Early Republic: The Case of the Federalist Clergy," in *Religion and American Politics from the Colonial Period to the 1980s*, ed. Mark Noll (New York: Oxford University Press, 1990) 62–63.

2

undermining "Christian Truth in the American mind." Those two, Adams charged, fired by ideas of infidelity from Europe, but beloved by popularity at home, attacked Christianity. More dangerous, Adams declared, was the shift in laws away from Christian principles, most notably that of operating the postal service on Sundays. He saw the "anti-Sabbath laws" as contrary to the nation's Christian founding.

Adams's arguments are those of Conservative political activists today known in popular media as the "Christian Right," who also claim that America was founded as a Christian nation, that the separation of church and state is a myth, and that today's secularists and liberals are to blame for understating or erasing religion from American history and culture. And, like Adams, Christian Right "historians," self-styled historians who are not educated in the discipline and do not adhere to the standards of historical scholarship, "prove" their claims through their own "inductive examination" of the founding documents. One, David Barton, repeats Adams's strained interpretation based on the Constitution's date. Another, John Eidsmoe, claims that the delegates who drafted the Constitution were inspired more by John Calvin than Enlightenment figures like John Locke and Baron de Montesquieu. Through selective quotations taken out of context and, in some instances, fabricated quotations, these "historians" rewrite the nation's founding. To support their claims, they cite James Madison among others as one of the principle architects of the "Christian State."

James Madison responded to Adams's claims in a way that answers the claims of those today who make similar claims. Adams sent a copy of his sermon to Madison soliciting comments from the "Father of the Constitution." Madison began his reply with a historical survey of church-state connections, stating that in pre-Reformation Europe, under "the Papal System, Government and Religion are in a manner consolidated, & that is found to be the worst of Govts." Although they allowed a "liberal toleration," Protestants were little better than Catholics, subscribing to the notion "that Religion could not be preserved without the support of Govt. nor Govt be supported with an established religion [and] that there must be at least an alliance of some sort between them." Madison noted that it was in America that "by successive relaxations" church and state were separated "without any evidence of disadvantage either to Religion or good Government." He pointed out that the separation of church and state had not hampered the growth and vitality of religion as some had feared, maintaining instead that "the lapse of time now more than 50 years since the legal support of Religion was withdrawn sufficiently prove [sic] that it does not need the support of Govt. and it will scarcely be contended that Government has suffered by the exemption of Religion from its cognizance, or its pecuniary aid." Madison added, "I must admit moreover that it may not be easy, in every possible case, to trace the line of separation between the rights of religion and the Civil authority." While some have argued that Madison's metaphor of a "line" instead of Thomas Jefferson's "wall" meant that he had softened his position on the separation of church and state, Madison made it clear in the next sentence that his views on the subject had not changed over the past fifty-six years from when he first fought for separation in Virginia in 1776. "The tendency to a usurpation on one side or the other, or to a corrupting coalition or alliance between them," he concluded, "will be best guarded agst by an *entire abstinance* of the Govt. from interference *in any way whatever*, [author's emphasis] beyond the necessity of preserving public order,

& protecting each sect agst. trespasses on its legal rights by others."[3]

Writing years after retiring from public life, Madison reaffirmed his commitment to church-state separation and noted that religion flourished in America's free market of religion. He rejected the notion of a "Christian Government," stressing the positive results of the separation of church and state that were evident following ratification of the Constitution. He noted that "the number, the industry, and the morality of the priesthood, and the devotion of the people have been manifestly increased by the total separation of the church from the state."[4]

Evangelicals in the "lived past" of the Revolutionary Era were strong supporters of Madison and the fight for the separation of church and state. Baptists and Presbyterians, two of the fastest growing denominations in the Revolutionary Era, led the battle for separation in Virginia, and then worked tirelessly to disestablish religion in Connecticut and Massachusetts. The Baptist minister John Leland was a leading advocate arguing that government should have no more involvement in religion than it should in mathematics. Confident in their ability to win converts and gain new members in the free marketplace of religion, evangelicals wanted no government support or interference. Thus, in the founding of the American republic, evan-

---

[3] Gaillard Hunt, ed., *The Writings of James Madison, Comprising His Public Papers and His Private Correspondence, Including His Numerous Letters and Documents Now for the First Time Printed*, 9 vols. (New York: G.P. Putnam's Sons, 1900) 9:484–87. For an excellent treatment of the history of the separation of church and state, see Daniel Dreisbach, *Thomas Jefferson and the Wall of Separation Between Church and State* (New York: NYU Press, 2003).

[4] Hunt, ed., *The Writings of James Madison*, 8:432.

gelicals joined enlightened liberals in demanding that church and state be separated.

For 190 years the vast majority of Americans accepted the separation of church and state as the surest safeguard of religious freedom. Many religious leaders, including Conservative Evangelicals, endorsed separation. Prominent Southern Baptist minister W.A. Criswell, pastor of the influential First Baptist Church of Dallas, Texas, invoked the principle of separation of church and state in opposing John F. Kennedy in the 1960 Presidential race. Fearing that Kennedy's Catholicism would divide his loyalty between Washington and Rome, Criswell declared unequivocally, "It is written in our country's constitution that church and state must be, in this nation, forever separate and free." Writing in the journal *United Evangelical Action*, Criswell declared that religious faith must be free and voluntary, adding that "there can be no proper union of church and state."[5] At the same time, Kennedy defended himself by invoking the same principle of separation of church and state. He confessed that his personal religious beliefs were those of the Catholic Church, but he added that his political commitment was to the United States Constitution. Speaking before the Houston Ministerial Association on 12 September, a largely hostile audience, Kennedy declared,

> I believe in an America where the separation of church and state is absolute—where no Catholic prelate would tell the president (should he be Catholic) how to act, and no Protestant minister would tell his parishioners for whom to vote—where no church or church school is granted any public funds or political preference—and where no man is denied public office merely because his religion differs

---

[5] W.A. Criswell, "Religious Freedom and the Presidency," *United Evangelical Action* 19 (September 1960): 9–10.

from the president who might appoint him or the people who might elect him.[6]

Thus, in 1960, persons on both sides of the highly charged political fight agreed that the separation of church and state was a fundamental principle adopted to protect both civil and religious freedoms. Like most Americans since the nation's founding, Criswell and Kennedy, though poles apart in their theological and political views, embraced the principle as a cherished bulwark of freedom.

Then in 1979 a group calling itself the Moral Majority renounced church-state separation and sought to do just what Madison feared: organize itself into a loose-knit political coalition, mobilize a majority of like-thinking Americans, and impose its religious views on the nation. Ironically, one of its founders, Baptist minister Jerry Falwell, had as recently as the mid-1960s declared that "preachers are not called upon to be politicians, but soul winners. Nowhere are we commissioned to reform the externals."[7] Then a decade later, in an about-face, he urged fellow evangelicals to "take back" the country from "secular humanists" who sought to remove religion from the public square. From that beginning, Conservative Evangelicals have emerged as a powerful political force in American electoral politics. Frequently described as the "Christian Right," the most Conservative Christian activists operate

---

[6] See address of Senator John F. Kennedy to the Greater Houston Ministerial Association, 12 September 1960, posted on the JFK Library website: http://www.jfklibrary.org/Research/Ready-Reference/JFK-Speeches/Address-of-Senator-John-F-Kennedy-to-the-Greater-Houston-Ministerial-Association.aspx (accessed 10 August 2012).

[7] Cited in Amy Sullivan, "The Good Fight: How Much Longer Can the Religious Left Remain Politically Neutral?" *Washington Monthly*, March 2005, viewed online at www.washingtonmonthly.com/features/2005. Site accessed August 20, 2013.

from the extreme right wing of the Republican Party, and they have challenged the party to take on such moral issues as school prayer, abortion, and homosexuality. At its best, the Christian Right stands in the reform traditions of the nineteenth century, when evangelicals operated in the newly formed Republican Party to fight for the abolition of slavery and a return to republican virtue. At its worst, it labels all who oppose it as anti-Christian and anti-religion. Indeed, the Christian Right sees itself engaged in a culture war for the very soul of the country.

Falwell was hardly alone in reversing his position. In 1980, Criswell also did an about-face on the separation of church and state. At a Texas rally for Ronald Reagan, Falwell introduced Criswell as "the Protestant pope of this generation," an ironic designation for a fervent anti-Catholic Protestant. When introducing Reagan, Criswell welcomed the Republican candidate "on behalf of the governor of Texas, the people of Dallas, and thirty million evangelicals." Reagan responded with his oft-quoted remark, "Now I know this is a nonpartisan gathering...so I know you can't endorse me, but I only brought that up because I want you to know that I endorse you and what you are doing." Then, on 24 August 1980, at the Republican National Convention, Criswell made his conversion complete and public: "I believe this notion of the separation of church and state was the figment of some infidel's imagination."[8]

Why did these modern-day Conservative Evangelicals diverge from the stance taken by evangelicals during the Revolutionary Era? Part of the explanation is a loss of confidence. Secular ideas and institutions have found favor

---

[8] Quoted in Richard Pierard, "Religion and the 1984 Election Campaign," *Review of Religious Research* 27 (December 1985): 104–105.

among millions of Americans who expect more from science and the marketplace than religion in solving their problems. Further, Americans increasingly turn to government for services once provided almost exclusively by the church, including educational, medical, and welfare programs. Rather than considering that their message and/or their strategy might be responsible for the decline in religious influence, the Christian Right blames others for their fate: liberals, secularists, government officials, scientists, and historians. And in recent years they have tried through partisan politics to do what the Constitution bans: the imposition of a religious test.

What follows takes issue with the Christian Right, a term used frequently, and, therefore, in need of defining. It is a pejorative term that has become a part of America's adversarial system of partisan politics where opponents seek to reduce each other with loaded labels and name-calling. The Christian Right itself employs such pejorative terms as "liberals" or "secularists" or "Socialists" to label their political adversaries. Christian Right is somewhat misleading because it suggests a monolithic coalition of like-minded people. In fact, the Christian Right is an amalgam of groups whose composition changes according to the issue being advocated or attacked. With those qualifications, however, the term Christian Right has entered the vocabulary of American political culture and recognizes the considerable success the coalition has had in advancing its causes and candidates at the local, state, and federal levels. Although an imperfect term, it is used in this book to designate advocates of a specific view of the founding and the founders.

To be clear, this book has no quarrel with Conservative Evangelicals, either from the founding period or from today. They are part of the rich religious diversity that comprises the free marketplace of religion in America. Because of separation of church and state, there is no official religion, nor does any group enjoy government support. Rather, all groups are voluntary organizations financed by their supporters. Conservative Evangelicals, like most religious coalitions, are a diverse lot, some identified with specific denominations and others operating as independent congregations. As religious groups the "truth" of their beliefs is of importance only to their members. If others in the marketplace of religion find their teachings "false," they are free to point out their "errors" or stay away from them.

This book also has no quarrel with the Christian Coalition or other Conservative political organizations who strive to sway American politics by seeking the election of candidates sympathetic to their aims and advocating for public policies they deem important. Thousands of lobby groups and political activist organizations attempt to influence American politics at the local, state, and federal level. Most are advocates for various secular interests, but many are driven by religious and moral concerns. All groups, including religious advocates, who enter the political arena, are partisans and their actions are regarded as such. That means that religious coalitions who claim to represent universal religious beliefs or America's religious heritage can expect to be treated as partisans advocating a specific set of claims and positions opposed by religionists and secularists who hold different beliefs.

This book, however, does have a quarrel with those self-styled "historians" sympathetic to the Christian Right who are on a mission to rewrite the nation's founding. Specifically, they make their case through compiling selective quotations taken out of context and through faulty logic that offers the founders' personal religious beliefs as "proof" that the framers formed a Christian state. What to call these revisionists is problematic. They do not qualify as professional historians either by education or practice; nonetheless, they make bald assertions about the nation's past while demonizing academic historians who, they charge, have conspired to distort or remove religious influences in America. Further, they use the term "historian" self-referentially. In this book they are referred to as revisionists or Christian Right "historians," with quotation marks distinguishing them from trained, professional historians who follow rigorous rules of investigation.

These revisionists make three claims that they support with selective evidence and specious logic. First, they claim that the United States was founded as a Christian state based on biblical and Protestant (read, Calvinist) principles. To substantiate that assertion, they gather every quotation of the founders favorable to Christian beliefs while ignoring quotations and actions that favor keeping church and state separate. Then they assert that it logically follows that these Christian men created a Christian state. But, of course, that is faulty logic: because one was a professing Christian does not mean he advocated a Christian America. Second they claim that modern-day "liberals" and "secularists" who dominate academic history departments have deliberately tried to erase the influence of religion on American history. They deny any authority of secular thought in the Revolutionary Period, ignoring or minimizing the influence of Enlightenment, Whig, or Liberal ideas, self-referential terms that the founders themselves frequently used. And, third, they claim that separation of church and state is a liberal/secularist myth, pointing out that the phrase does not appear in any of the founding documents. Here they use an argument of silence to make their case, while dismissing a similar argument made by others who point out that the terms "Jesus," "Christ," and "Christian" are also absent in the founding documents.

The revisionists claim that they not only are the defenders of America's Christian heritage, they are warriors engaged in nothing short of a culture war. Whether there is a war is debatable; however, there is, nonetheless, much controversy over the claims put forward by the revisionists. And, as Lutheran church historian Theodore Tappert stated in 1942, "Controversies stimulate historical investigation but produce propaganda."[9] The aim of this book is to separate propaganda and myth from history. Our point of departure is to turn assertion into question and then put those questions to the historical record as interpreted within the context of the nation's founding. Was America founded as a Christian republic, and if so, what was the intended nature of that republic and upon what principles did it rest? If secularists and liberals challenged religious claims about the nature, operation, and purpose of the republic, when, how, and why did they make their challenges? And, how are we to regard the separation of church and state in America? Is it a founding principle cherished by the framers of the Constitution? Or, is it a myth foisted on Americans by latter-day liberals and secularists?

In answering these questions, evangelicals have offered and continue to offer different answers. To today's most vocal Conservative Evangelicals, separation of church and state is a myth perpetrated by latter-day liberals. However, that position is undercut by evangelicals of the Revolutionary Era who fought hard for the doctrine of separation as a constitutional safeguard of religious liberty. Thus, in constructing their "usable past" wherein sepa-

---

[9] Theodore Tappert, "The Muhlenberg Tradition in the Nineteenth Century," *Lutheran Church Quarterly* 15 (1942): 398.

ration of church and state is a liberal myth and not a constitutional principle, today's Conservative Evangelicals confront Revolutionary Evangelicals whose "lived past" was dedicated to keeping church and state separate in order to guarantee religious freedom. Unlike today's Conservative Evangelicals who seek government support for their cause, Revolutionary Evangelicals agreed with James Madison that the Church, even under its bloodiest persecution, needed no state support for carrying out its mission. God alone was sufficient. Further, they welcomed the free marketplace of religion created by separation and were confident that they and their message would thrive if the state had nothing to do with religion.

This book argues that the testimony of revolutionary evangelicals as well as enlightened statesmen makes a convincing case that the separation of church and state was indeed a vital constitutional principle of 1776. It was evangelicals who joined with enlightened liberals to fight for disestablishment, first in the path-breaking case in Virginia, and then in state after state until Massachusetts became the last to separate church and state in 1833. Any suggestion that separation is a figment of twentieth-century liberal minds ignores the historical record of the Revolutionary Era, including that depicting the central role of evangelicals in the fight for separation of church and state.

The book challenges the revisionists' "usable past," which says more about Conservative Evangelicals today than about the founding era. The first chapter is a polemic aimed at the revisionists of the Christian Right who are unanimous in demonizing "academic historians" as tools of secular and liberal perspectives. Although revisionists are not educated in the discipline of history and violate every tenet of sound historical investigation, they persist in representing their work as "history." Chapter 1 judges their efforts against the standards of scholarship that academic historians follow. In particular, it examines the selection and use of evidence by which Christian Right "historians" make their claims. And, it looks at the logic and context by which they interpret the past.

The remaining four chapters are a historical investigation into questions sparked by the specific claims of the Christian Right "historians." Chapter 2 examines the claim that America was founded as a Christian state. While evidence from 1787 does not support that claim for the creation of the United States, there is an example of a Christian commonwealth created at the time of early English settlement. Massachusetts Bay Colony was conceived of as a Christian state under a covenant between God and the people of Massachusetts and explicitly organized according to biblical precepts. So it represents a model for the kind of state that the Christian Right advocates. Upon close analysis, however, it was not the kind of Christian state that would appeal to Americans today, including the Christian Right. It privileged orthodoxy over freedom, uniformity over diversity, and conformity over dissent. Indeed, it was short-lived in large part because dissenters who lived in the colony agitated for greater individual freedom and less state control. In claiming that the U.S. was founded as a Christian state, the Christian Right "historians" conflate early colonial settlement with the early republic. They fail to account for change over time, over the 150 or so years that separated early English settlement and the Revolutionary period. They, therefore, fail to see the triumph of freedom over orthodoxy, diversity over uniformity, and dissent over conformity.

Chapter 3 turns to the claim that present-day "secularists" and "liberals" have distorted the place and importance of religion in America's past. By examining the eighteenth-century evangelical revival known as the Great Awakening and the set of ideas known as the American Enlightenment, one sees that from its early development, American culture was both deeply sacred and deeply secular. To reduce America's history to one or the other is to distort the narrative. Awakened and Enlightened Americans differed sharply in their worldviews, but they also shared similar interests; they both challenged received authority, including that of the church, and both elevated the place of the individual in American life. So secular, as well as sacred, ideas shaped the United States from its birth, and did not emerge only in the present age as the Christian Right insists. This chapter shows the stamp of Enlightenment ideas on the Declaration of Independence, and while the influence of Natural Theology is readily evident on the document, only the most strained reading renders the declaration a Christian work as the Christian Right contends.

Chapter 4 takes up the question of separation of church and state by examining the place of religion in the earliest state constitutions. It looks first at Massachusetts's constitutional settlement of state-supported religion with religious toleration of dissenters. Then it examines the opposition to religious establishment in Virginia and the insistence by evangelicals and Enlightened leaders to guarantee religious freedom and not merely grant religious toleration. It ends with the contagion of liberty in the new republic that led to the disestablishment of religion in Massachusetts and Connecticut, so that, by 1833, no state had a state-supported religion, although some continued to impose a religious test on officeholders.

Chapter 5 looks at the question of the separation of church and state in the federal Constitution. The Christian Right is correct in pointing out that the phrase does not appear in any of the founding documents, but they fail to see the importance of the principle of separation for curbing power and safeguarding liberty. Just as separation divided power between the states and the central government and spread power over the three branches of government, it also kept church and state from commingling and thus corrupting each other as they had repeatedly done throughout history. By putting religion on a voluntary, instead of a state-supported, basis, the founders created a free marketplace of religion, a competitive place whereby the various churches could check any single group from imposing its will on the whole nation, and an innovative place whereby new religions are spawned and old ones adapt and change to increase their appeal to more people.

This book is intended for the educated and interested reader who is not a specialist in American religious history. It is a synthetic work in that it draws upon previous works that the author has written as well as the wealth of scholarship in the field. When quoting those from the founding era, primary documents are cited and interpreted within historical context. That is, rather than reading present-day views back into the past, it looks at how the founders viewed the place of religion in the new republic. Such an approach keeps the focus on the founders' actions and the kind of state they crafted. Frequently, however, quotes of Christian Right protagonists are traced to websites. The Christian Right has made effective use of the Internet to convey their message to the broadest audience.

In 1832, Jasper Adams wanted a closer connection between church and state because he worried about religious and moral decline in the United States. Evangelicals, including Baptists, Methodists, Presbyterians, Disciples of Christ, and some from Adams's own Episcopal Church, disagreed. At the time, they were leading a great revival that brought tens of thousands of new members to their congregations. In other words, they were doing very well in the religious marketplace and wanted no government support or interference at all.

1

Christian Right "Historians": Fabricating a "Usable Past"

To Conservative members of the Texas School Board, American textbooks distort the history of the nation's founding by failing to recognize its Christian underpinning. One member, David Bradley, a Conservative from Beaumont who works in real estate, says that he rejects "the notion by the left of a constitutional separation of church and state." Other members object to "liberal" textbooks that depict the American Revolution as having a "secular nature." Cynthia Dunbar, a lawyer from Richmond, expressed her view that the nation was founded on Christian beliefs, and she disapproves of the undue attention given Thomas Jefferson and the Enlightenment in mainstream textbooks. Conservatives do not care for Jefferson, who is credited with coining the phrase, "separation of church and state," and who is seen as a strong proponent of the Enlightenment.[1] They vow to replace existing textbooks with those from which students can learn about the United States founded as a Christian nation.

---

[1] See "Texas Conservatives Win Curriculum Change," *New York Times,* 12 March 2010.

In the past two decades, a number of self-styled "historians" have undertaken the task of rewriting American history to undo and correct the distorted narratives of secularists and misguided Christian liberals. According to these Conservative Evangelicals, America was founded as a Christian nation because a group of Christian men instilled its formative documents with Christian principles. They are determined to set the historical record straight by providing Americans with the "true" history of the faith of America's founding.

At the forefront of the crusade to rewrite American history is David Barton, who calls himself a historian but has no formal education in the discipline of history. A religious studies major at Oral Roberts University, Barton reflects the Fundamentalist perspective of the institution's founder, and as former vice-chairman of the Texas Republican Party, he is an influential partisan in the right wing of the party. In his speeches and publications, Barton rails against "liberals" and "secularists," often using the most outrageous language to attack his opponents. He has called President Obama "America's Most Biblically-Hostile U.S. President," claiming that Obama exhibits "preferential deference for Islam's activities and positions, including letting his Islamic advisors guide and influence his hostility toward people of Biblical faith." And Barton attacks members of the Republican Party who dare exercise independent judgment and vote against measures dear to the Christian Right. When four Republicans in the New York assembly voted against an anti-gay marriage proposal, Barton blasted them on his WallBuilders Live website: "No disrespect to our Native American friends, but this is where you hang a bloody scalp over the gallery rail. You hang these four Republican scalps over the Senate rail and every other Republican senator looks up and sees those scalps and says, 'my gosh, I'll be hanging up there beside them if I don't stay with this pro-family stuff.' And that's exactly what has to happen."[2]

Barton's partisan perspective and agenda are found on the website for WallBuilders, an organization he founded in 1989 for promoting his right-wing religious and political views, not only on current American life, but on the way American history is interpreted, written, and taught. He claims that WallBuilders is "dedicated to presenting America's forgotten history and heroes, with an emphasis on the moral, religious, and constitutional foundation on which America was built—a foundation which, in recent years, has been seriously attacked and undermined." Barton takes his inspiration from the Bible:

> In the Old Testament book of *Nehemiah*, the nation of Israel rallied together in a grassroots movement to help rebuild the walls of Jerusalem and thus restore stability, safety, and a promising future to that great city. We have chosen this historical concept of "rebuilding the walls" to represent allegorically the call for citizen involvement in rebuilding our nation's foundations. As Psalm 11:3 reminds us, "If the foundations be destroyed, what shall the righteous do?"[3]

Barton identifies secular academic historians as the villains who have distorted American history. He declares,

> For over three centuries, historians presented American history from a broad perspective, but in the 1960s historical writers widely embraced what today is called the "economic view of American history" whereby economic causes are the primary and almost singular emphasis of

---

[2] Barton's quotations are taken from his WallBuilders website: http://www.wallbuilders.com/libissuesarticles.asp?id=106938 (accessed 10 August 2012).

[3] See http://www.wallbuilders.com/ABTOverview.asp (accessed 10 August 2010).

study. Consequently, students study only "taxation without representation" when they examine the Declaration of Independence rather than important civil, governmental, and moral principles addressed in that document.[4]

This chapter examines the history fabricated by Barton and other self-styled historians engaged in creating a "usable past," that is, one they craft to reflect and validate their cause. First, it looks at the men themselves, their educational backgrounds, especially their grounding in the discipline of history, their religious and political affiliations and viewpoints, and the claims that they make. Second, it critiques the methodologies that Barton and others use to make their historical claims, especially how they select and use evidence. And, third, it contrasts the fabrication and investigation of history.

Christian Right "Historians"?

Barton is neither the only nor the first person from the Christian Right who has waged war against academic historians. Co-founder of the Moral Majority, Timothy LaHaye, is a prolific writer who has been on a crusade for the past thirty years to cast America as a Christian nation. His rise to national leadership as a self-proclaimed historian from the Christian Right came in 1979 when President Jimmy Carter invited a group of Conservative Evangelicals to the White House for breakfast. Among those included were Jerry Falwell, Oral Roberts, Jim Bakker, Charles Stanley, and LaHaye. Evangelicals had helped elect Carter in 1976, but he had lost much of their support because of policy positions deemed too "liberal" and anti-evangelical. Carter had, for example, supported the Equal Rights Amendment, a stance that alienated many Conservatives

---

[4] Ibid.

who thought it undermined the ideal of the Christian family. And he had insisted that federal civil rights laws apply to private Christian schools, a position that some Conservative Evangelicals interpreted as hostile to their religion. Carter tried to assure those gathered for breakfast that he was a committed evangelical who was pro-family. LaHaye was unconvinced, noting that, among other things, Carter was vague on the controversial question of abortion. Afterward, he proclaimed: "We had a man in the White House who professed to be a Christian, but didn't understand how un-Christian his administration was."[5]

LaHaye became a leading figure in a coalition of Conservative Christians who sought to defeat Carter's bid for re-election in 1980. While exulting in the election of Ronald Reagan and boasting of their role in his victory, the Christian Right aimed at more than winning an election; they wished to change the nation's political culture, which, they charged, had been subverted by "secular humanists" who had removed God from the public square. LaHaye and others argued that the nation was founded as a "Christian Nation," that the founders viewed religion as important to public life, and that the prevailing notion of "the separation of church and state" was a myth created by liberal judges.

To set the historical record straight, in 1984, LaHaye published *Faith of Our Founding Fathers*. A central aim in his revisionist history was to "prove [that] the overwhelming majority of the Founding Fathers of this nation were raised in and believed in the Christian faith." In his treatment of George Washington, LaHaye asserted that the first President was a "devout believer in Jesus Christ" who

---

[5] Cited in Barry Hankins, *American Evangelicals: A Contemporary History of a Mainstream Religious Movement* (Lanham MD: Rowman and Littlefield Publisher, 2009) 144.

"accepted Him as His Lord and Savior." Viewing Washington as a born-again evangelical, LaHaye declared that, if Washington were living today, "he would freely identify with the Bible-believing branch of evangelical Christianity."[6] LaHaye's readers (and they are legion: his *Left Behind* series has sold more than fifty million copies) accept his interpretation as an article of faith. To them, much is at stake. If America was founded as a Christian nation, then surely its leading lights were devout Christians who made Christianity an important part of their governance. So LaHaye and others in the Christian Right have constructed a past that attests to the evangelical piety of such founding luminaries as Washington, John Adams, Thomas Jefferson, and James Madison.

LaHaye's credentials as a historian are as thin as Barton's. He received a Bachelor of Arts degree from Bob Jones University, a Fundamentalist college located in Greenville, South Carolina. Students and faculty subscribe to a creed developed by its founder, Bob Jones, who set forth the essential fundamentals of faith that every Christian must believe. The creed reads as follows:

> I believe in the inspiration of the Bible (both the Old and the New Testaments); the creation of man by the direct act of God; the incarnation and virgin birth of our Lord and Saviour, Jesus Christ; His identification as the Son of God; His vicarious atonement for the sins of mankind by the shedding of His blood on the cross; the resurrection of His body from the tomb; His power to save men from sin; the new birth through the regeneration by the Holy Spirit; and the gift of eternal life by the grace of God.[7]

---

[6] Timothy LaHaye, *Faith of Our Founding Fathers: A Comprehensive Study of America's Christian Foundation* (Google eBooks, 1994) np.

[7] See creed at Bob Jones University website: http://www.bju.edu/about-bju/creed.php (accessed 10 August 2012).

Every religious institution enjoys the right to define its beliefs; that right is not contested. The point here is that one who sees the world through a Fundamentalist prism cannot interpret the past as anything but a Christian narrative.

A few years after graduating in 1950, LaHaye moved to California where he became a pastor and political activist for Conservative causes. He was part of the post-World War II migration from the South to the West Coast, and there he became a key figure in the rise of the Conservative political movement that encouraged millions of Conservative Christians to join the Republican Party, culminating in the election of Ronald Reagan as California governor in 1967. Then in the late 1970s, LaHaye organized a grassroots movement called Californians for Biblical Morality to mobilize Conservative Evangelicals to elect Reagan President. He explained his motivation: "I realized that we Evangelical Christians, and that was a big broad group, had a concern for the moral decline of America and the rise of depravity. So we pulled together two hundred and forty-one ministers in Los Angeles and I shared the burden to them and we started our organization." LaHaye proudly recalls how he encouraged Reagan to run: "I had the audacity to write him a two page letter as to why he should run for Governor of the State of California, and after eight years in that capacity that would qualify him to run for President of the United States." And he did not regret prodding Reagan, whom he regards as, "my very favorite President in over one hundred years—the greatest President in American history." After Reagan's victory, LaHaye led social Conservatives in organizing the Council for National Policy (1981), a political action group that envisioned America as locked in a moral war with clear-cut sides. Again, LaHaye explained the opposition: "There is a philosophy that starts without God and ends up persecuting men: it's called socialism. And there is a philosophy of God that loves God and loves his fellow man and God wants to use him and he fosters freedom."[8]

Just as LaHaye was determined to win America for the Conservative cause, he was equally determined to rewrite American history in a Conservative key. He made the link explicit: "When we talk about re-taking America, we don't want to take it, we want America to return to the values of the Founding Fathers," and that meant identifying those values by creating a "usable past," that is, one that linked the founders with today's Republican Party. Thus, LaHaye's account of the country's beginning is that of a Fundamentalist Christian and a partisan for the extreme right wing of the Republican Party.

Another leading Christian Right "historian," John Eidsmoe, agrees with Barton and LaHaye that the new republic founded in 1776 and constituted in 1787 was established explicitly as a Christian nation. Like them, Eidsmoe is at the far right of both the theological and political spectrums. After earning a bachelor's degree from St. Olaf's College and a J.D. degree from the University of Iowa, Eidsmoe redirected his education at some of the most Conservative institutions. He received a master's degree in Divinity from Lutheran Brethren Seminary and a master's in Biblical Studies from Dallas Theological Seminary. Then he got a Doctor of Ministry degree from Oral Roberts University. An ordained pastor in the Association of Free Lutheran Congregations, he has spent much of his career as a law professor at such institutions as Oral Roberts and Faulkner University in Montgomery, Alabama. He has championed many ultraconservative causes, including the

---

[8] See http://www.cfnp.org/page.aspx?pid=180 (accessed 29 June 2012).

battle to put the Ten Commandments on public display at federal courthouses. He believes that feminists "violate the normal order" that God put in place for husbands to head households, that "homosexuality invites the judgment of God upon all of society," that gays will turn the military into a "cesspool of immorality,"[9] and that public education is brainwashing students to believe in secularism and evolution. In 2010, speaking at a rally celebrating Alabama's secession from the Union, Eidsmoe not only defended secession but claimed that Jefferson Davis and John C. Calhoun understood the Constitution better than Abraham Lincoln. His extreme views on states' rights resulted in his being disinvited to a political rally by Tea Party organizers who thought his position was too divisive.

Eidsmoe's revision of the founding of America is set forth in his book, *Christianity and the Constitution: The Faith of Our Founding Fathers* (1987). There, Eidsmoe claims that Calvin, not Montesquieu or Locke, inspired the delegates that drafted the Constitution, and that they founded the government on biblical principles. The foreword to the book asserts:

> Dr. Eidsmoe shows clearly how most of our founding fathers were not secular men, as we often hear today. He explains how the influence of Calvinism gave rise to our republican form of government. He also documents how our founding fathers embodied several biblical principles in the Constitution. This book is recommended for anyone who wants to learn about our nation's truly Christian heritage, which has been virtually expunged by the secular revisionists.[10]

---

[9] John Eidsmoe, *Gays & Guns: The Case Against Homosexuals in the Military* (Lafayette LA: Huntington House Publisher, 1993) 70–71.

[10] See Foreword to John Eidsmoe, *Christianity and the Constitution: The Faith of Our Founding Fathers* (Ada MI: Baker Academic, 1995).

More than a history, *Christianity and the Constitution* is a call for Conservatives to become politically active and elect Conservative Christians who will demand that the country base its laws on biblical principles, principles Eidsmoe insists were those that guided the founders.

One more evangelical historian merits mention in the Conservative Christian effort to revise U.S. history as the story of a nation founded as a Christian republic. Like the others, William Federer was not educated as a historian; rather, he received a degree in accounting from St. Louis University. After graduation, he became a real estate agent before becoming active in Conservative causes. In 2000 he was unsuccessful in his bid as the Republican candidate to unseat Richard Gephardt from the U.S. House of Representatives. Federer is active as a speaker and writer on Conservative topics and is best known for his encyclopedia of quotations from historical figures. Like Barton, LaHaye, and Eidsmoe, he wishes to "restore" religion to the story of America's past, and he thinks one of the best ways to do that is to compile a list of every quote that the founders made on the subject of religion. To him, the long list that he generated "proves" that the founders were Christian men motivated by Christian principles to found a Christian society.

To summarize, these revisionists have several characteristics in common. First, they are not educated as historians, and they do not practice history. That is, they do not investigate the past on its own terms, seeking to understand historical events and movements and figures within context. Rather, they commit the cardinal sin of presentism, the practice of assigning to the past the biases and meanings of the present. Second, they are religious and political activists for causes that place them on the far right of the ideological spectrum. Third, they are firmly entrenched in the right wing of the Republican Party. Fourth, they portray academic historians as villains, secularists, and liberals who deliberately distort history by minimizing or criticizing religion as a positive influence in American life. And, fifth, they are determined to rewrite American history in a way that reflects their own values and principles.

A Critique of the Fabricators' Work

Those determined to rewrite history to reflect their own religious and political views start with the premise that academic historians have either omitted or distorted the role of religion in American history. They make sweeping statements that give the impression that academic historians act in concert and have conspired to remove religion from their texts. A cursory examination of the catalogs of university presses over the past several decades reveal just the opposite. Far from acting in unison, academic historians have published a broad spectrum of works illuminating America's past with hundreds of works underscoring the role and influence of religion on American history and culture. And, far from writing a single narrative or a variation on a single theme, academic historians conduct lively debates with each other about the country's history. There is no single dominant line of interpretation. Even in the 1960s, Marxism provided historians with but one of many interpretative templates for understanding the past, and those who saw the past through an economic prism differed with each other on such questions as economic determinism and the source and influence of cultural phenomenon on the course of history. Although Marxist historians made a significant contribution to the understanding of American history, especially the rise and influence of capital, the mobilization of labor, and the

28

development of markets, economic historians never dominated and always found their work challenged by other academic historians who warned against economic reductionism. At the same time, an equally vigorous group of scholars emphasized cultural influences rather than economic ones as most important in shaping American life. Those historians frequently put religion at the center of their analysis. Hundreds of titles emerged on such subjects as Puritanism, religious diversity, religious freedom, and religious revivals (especially the Great Awakening), as well as religious figures who shaped the country's past. Arguments that academic historians have ignored religion in writing U.S. history are aimed at creating a straw man erected in order to then be deftly cut down.

The writing of history by academic historians is an ongoing conversation about America's past. Scholars familiarize themselves with what others have written, and they situate their own publications within the existing literature. On the other hand, those who fabricate the past show little or no understanding of the body of historical writing, and, rather than engaging in an honest and open exchange of ideas, simply dismiss the work of academic historians.

One way to assess the quality of the histories produced by Barton and like-minded individuals is to evaluate those works against the standards of historical scholarship. Paul Harvey of the University of California is an academic historian who focuses primarily on American religious history. A prolific writer, he adheres to the highest standards of historical scholarship, and he is disturbed by those who fabricate the past in the name of explaining it. He says that David Barton's project is not a historical one but rather one of "ideological entrepreneurialism," by which he means that Barton is more interested in selling his

Conservative ideas to voters and officeholders in order to influence public policy than he is in historical scholarship. As Harvey puts it, "Barton's intent is not to produce 'scholarship,' but to influence public policy. He simply is playing a different game than worrying about scholarly credibility, his protestations to the contrary notwithstanding. His game is to inundate public policy makers (including local and state education boards as well as Congress) with ideas packaged as products that will move policy." And to the many Conservative devotees who agree with him, all the sound scholarship that can be mustered will not convince them that Barton is wrong in his attack on academic historians. Barton does not worry about the lack of scholarly credentials, because he knows that his readers agree with him that academics are wrong-headed liberals who cannot be trusted.[11]

Nonetheless, it is important to challenge fabricators of the past who try to pass off their work as the result of historical scholarship. Barton, LaHaye, Eidsmoe, and Federer all claim to base their conclusions about America's founding on thorough research and convincing evidence. If they are posing as historians, then their work should be subjected to the same vetting process that academic historians face when they submit and publish their scholarship. What follows is a step-by-step evaluation of the fabricators' method of writing history.

Good history begins with questions, not answers. If historians are relevant, they must ask questions that are

---

[11] See Paul Harvey, "Selling the Idea of a Christian Nation: David Barton's Alternate Intellectual Universe," posted at http://www.religiondispatches.org/archive/politics/4589/selling_the_id ea_of_a_christian_nation%3A_david_barton%E2%80%99s_alternate_intelle ctual_universe/ (accessed 30 June 2012).

informed by the present and that people today find engaging. For example, in the post-World War II period, the United States has fought a number of wars, but none of them declared by Congress, raising the question in the Johnson and Nixon administrations of "the imperial presidency." A number of historians then probed the past in search of precedents or explanations of how Presidents have used their war-making powers. The result was a number of works on such topics as Andrew Jackson's removal of the Eastern Indians despite a Supreme Court decision upholding the natives' claims to their land. Other works chronicle America's undeclared wars against the Barbary pirates when Thomas Jefferson committed American forces against Tripoli after attacks on American shipping. So historians find questions in the present and ask, how did we get to this point, or what are the origins of this movement, or how has this phenomenon changed over time? To be legitimate, the question must be one that is answered only after careful scrutiny of the historical record. While questions emanate in the present, they must be decided on the basis of evidence from the past considered within historical context.

Whether the United States was founded as a Christian state and whether or not the founders separated church and state are legitimate and important questions, questions that deserve thorough investigation. To answer those questions, a careful historian would conduct a methodical examination that would begin with a close study of the context of the founding of America. He or she would want to find out why delegates convened at Philadelphia in 1787. What problems did the country face, and why did the current constitution, the Articles of Confederation, not suffice? Next the investigator would want to know what the delegates knew about the theory and practice of constitution-making in history, or stated differently, what books did the delegates read about political theory and struggles? The answer to that question would provide a range of options that the delegates would have considered for framing the U.S. Constitution. The historian would want to explore the experiences that the delegates had had in crafting state constitutions, and what lessons they had learned, both positive and negative, from that experience. Next, the historian would want to study the plans various delegates put forth for revising the articles in order to get an idea of the preliminary ideas that set the agenda for debate within the convention. Then the investigator would want to read everything bearing on the convention: the political alignments that coalesced around each article, the most intractable issues, and the compromises reached to move the process on. Then he or she would want to explore the principles upon which the delegates agreed and the different meanings they assigned those principles based on regional, economic, and ideological interests. In addition to examining the delegates' ideas, the historian would want to pay close attention to their actions, especially regarding the question of religion. What powers, if any, did the delegates grant Congress respecting religion? How did they establish the relation between a citizen's religion and his or her civil rights? What importance did the delegates attach to religion in the new republic, and what was the relation between religion and the state? What was to be the place of religion in the early republic? Was it to operate with government support or by the voluntary support of church members? The historian would then want to see what various people had to say about the treatment of religion in the draft constitution, including what the delegates themselves said, what ratifiers said, and what interested citizens said. Finally, the investigator would want to assess how religion fared under the constitutional arrangement. Did it flourish? Did the founders' arrangement concerning the place of religion enable churches to operate as free, self-directed organizations, or, languish with insufficient support? Finally, how did religion serve the citizens of the new republic?

Rather than pursuing a systematic and comprehensive investigation of the nation's founding that begins with probing questions, the Christian Right "historians" start and end with preconceived answers. Writing out of deeply held convictions, they already know the "truth" of the past. Those ultraconservatives who assert that the United States was conceived of as a Christian nation have no doubts about the matter; their religious and political beliefs dictate the answers for them. They approach history, then, as sectarians and partisans seeking validation of their viewpoints, not as historians embarking on an investigation to find explanations that the past might have to offer. Thus they take a presentist view of the past. For them, the present does far more than inspire questions, it provides answers.

Presentist history is history by assertion, or pre-suppositional history. If one knows the conclusion before the investigation, then his or her case rests on existing beliefs, not on a careful and fair weighing of the evidence. In this case, the ultraconservative set of claims are assertions: (1) America is and has always been a Christian nation; (2) Present-day liberals and secularists have distorted that Christian heritage; and (3) The "separation of church and state" is a modern-day invention by the enemies of religion. However, if those claims are transformed into questions, they serve as the basis of a legitimate investigation of American religious history. Was the U.S. conceived of as a Christian republic? And that question invites several other lines of inquiry: What are the criteria by which a state is judged to be Christian? Does the Constitution and do the laws rest on Christian principles and authority? Do they adhere to biblical precepts? In establishing the republic in the period 1776–1779, did the founders consciously set about to create a religious commonwealth? Did they identify models from history of religious states such as "Catholic Spain" or "Islamist Constantinople"? In structuring the new republic and addressing the question of power, did they conceive of religion as a department of the state or did they view government as the primary supporter and defender of churches?

After raising questions to guide their historical investigation, historians must try to set aside their own biases and prejudices as they conduct their research. All people, and therefore all historians, have biases, and they must acknowledge and control them if their investigation is to produce a fair account of the past. Graduate students in history are constantly admonished to "check their biases" at the door before embarking on their research. Of course, no one can remove their prejudices completely, but they can make a conscious effort to control them.

Historians must also avoid tunnel vision. That is, they should not frame their investigation in such a narrowly focused way as to block out all possibilities except the one thing they are seeking. Eminent colonial historian at Yale, Edmund Morgan, used to tell his students about walking alongside a golf course paying no attention to golf balls that were hit and lost out of bounds. But, once the person starts looking for golf balls, perhaps to add to his or her collection or maybe to sell, the individual begins to spot golf balls all over the place. Morgan concluded that if one looks for golf balls, one finds golf balls. Similarly, if a historian looks for a particular thing, one finds that thing in the historical record to the exclusion of all else. As historians specialize as religious historians or economic historians or political historians, there is the danger that their research will be so focused as to find only what they seek. The result is often to overstate the importance of whatever is driving the study. If one, for example, believes that all of history is directed by God, then that person is going to find God at every moment in the past. However, the view that God's hand guides history is a theological belief, and it is not the historian's place to pass judgment on the validity of such a view. Rather, historians should restrict their explanation to how and when Americans have made such a claim and to what ends. To do more is to present oneself as a theologian and open oneself to a series of questions about one's particular theological perspective and authority.

One of the ways to separate good and bad history is to examine the selection and use of evidence. Is the research thorough and far-reaching? Does the investigator consider all the evidence relative to his or her question or only that which supports preconceived ideas? Barton and his cohorts attempt to make their case that America was conceived of as a Christian nation through compilations of quotes from the founders that express a religious viewpoint, or can be interpreted as such. By culling the historical record for religious quotes, they conclude that the case is self-evident: the founders were deeply religious and held religious convictions.

To fabricate a history that "proves" that America was conceived of as a Christian nation, Christian Right "historians" pile up quotes of the founders regarding religion. Historian of the Library of Congress, James Hutson, describes how compilers of quotes use or misuse them:

What better way to prove that the Founders were grounded and instructed by Christian principles than by calling the most important of them to the witness stand and letting them testify in their own words to the importance of Christianity in their lives? All quote book compilers employ this strategy, invariably focusing on Washington, Jefferson, Madison, Franklin, Adams, and a handful of lesser luminaries, culling statements from their writings that attest to the beneficent influence of Christianity on their lives and on the public welfare. On the basis of the evidence offered, they assume that only the most perverse reader could deny that Christianity was the formative force in the founding of the United States.[12]

Barton, Eidsmoe, LaHaye, and Federer assume that merely listing the founders' quotes on religion makes their case of America's founding as a Christian nation. But, while voicing religious views indicates personal convictions, it does not demonstrate that the founders' intended to create a Christian republic.

Moreover, Benjamin Franklin, one of the most iconic founders, urged caution in judging politicians by their professed religious utterances. He argued that power corrupts all politicians whether they are religious or irreligious. Further, he maintained that when politics and religion are mixed, the result is a particularly combustible threat to liberty. He wrote that "a little Religion, and a little Honesty, goes a great Way in Courts," meaning that they win enough confidence to mask the designs of a "Religious Man in Power." Franklin warned his readers to judge an officeholder not by his pious words, but by his honest behavior. He cited Whig writers John Trenchard and Thomas Gordon's *Cato* to warn about religious utterances

---

[12] James Hutson, ed., *The Founders on Religion: A Book of Quotations* (Princeton: Princeton University Press, 2005) ix–x.

from politicians. Many politicians, they wrote, "set up for wonderful pious Persons, while they were defying Almighty God, and plundering Men." They had seen an example of pious talk and evil behavior in the South Seas Bubble of the 1720s in which men deceived investors into putting their money in a scheme that rested more on inflated talk than on substantive prospects. In the end some speculators made money but thousands of investors lost their savings. Franklin's conclusion was that we must judge men not by their professions of faith, but by the "Whole of their Conduct, and the Effects of it."[13] The evangelical historians do not heed Franklin's warning.

In addition to the selective use of evidence, at least one Christian Right "historian" has been guilty of fabricating quotations to put in the founders' mouths words that support present-day ultraconservative views. Academic historians have long questioned David Barton's scholarship, charging him with, at best, superficial and sloppy "research," and, at worst, with making up evidence to fit his presupposed conclusions. He ignored such charges until 2000, when he decided to defend his actions, refusing to acknowledge that he had fabricated quotes, admitting instead that certain quotes were "unconfirmed." What follows is a sample of some of the more egregious examples of his fabrications. One should note that these are listed by Barton on his WallBuilders website with his designation of "unconfirmed":[14]

---

[13] Leonard Labaree, ed., *The Papers of Benjamin Franklin*, 40 vols. (New Haven CT: Yale University Press, 1959) 1:32.

[14] All of the following quotations, along with Barton's explanations, are found under "Unconfirmed Quotations," located at http://www.wallbuilders.com/libissuesarticles.asp?id=126 (accessed 30 June 2012).

"It cannot be emphasized too strongly or too often that this great nation was founded, not by religionists, but by Christians; not on religions, but on the gospel of Jesus Christ!"—Patrick Henry (unconfirmed).

Barton justified his fabrication by claiming, "Few could dispute that this quotation is consistent with Henry's life and character." He then deflects any wrongdoing from himself and attacks "secularists." He writes, "Interestingly, those who advocate a secular society today view Henry as an arch enemy," as if, even if the charge were true, that justifies the fabrication of evidence.

"It is impossible to rightly govern the world without God and the Bible."—George Washington (unconfirmed).

Again, Barton justifies his fabrication by stating that even though Washington did not utter or write these words, his other writings confirm that this is the sort of thing that Washington would say. He writes, "[Washington] often spoke on religious themes, to include the ruler of nations, the light of Revelation, and the symbiotic relationship between the Church and the state." For Barton, this constitutes "overwhelming evidence to support this thought as belonging to Washington." Again, he redirects blame toward "secularists": "Although the modern secularists avoid his numerous religious maxims, Washington's views on religion are easily documented."

"Our laws and our institutions must necessarily be based upon and embody the teachings of the Redeemer of mankind. It is impossible that it should be otherwise. In this sense and to this extent, our civilizations and our institutions are emphatically Christian."—*Holy Trinity v. U.S.* (Supreme Court) (inaccurate confirmed!—*Richmond v. Moore*, Illinois Supreme Court, 1883).

Note that in this instance, Barton admitted only that the quotation was inaccurate; moreover, he exclaimed that it was confirmed. He admitted that he had not consulted the court decision itself, but justified his error because "[t]his quotation appeared in many modern works, each attributing the wording to the U.S. Supreme Court's 1892 decision in the Holy Trinity case." In other words, he should not be held to blame for copying a mistake made by others. In admitting his error, he dismissed it as a typographical mistake: "After researching and being unable to locate this quote in that case, we concluded that it probably was a cut-and-paste typographical error, for several of the phrases do appear in that case."

> "We have staked the whole future of American civilization, not upon the power of government, far from it. We have staked the future of all of our political institutions upon the capacity of each and all of us to govern ourselves... according to the Ten Commandments of God."—James Madison (unconfirmed).

In explaining this fabrication, Barton returned to the notion that the quotation "sounds like something Madison would say." Barton wrote,

> While these words have been the most controversial of all unconfirmed quotes, they are consistent with Madison's thoughts on religion and government. They are consistent because the key idea being communicated is self-government, not religious laws or establishments. Our future rests upon the ability of all to govern themselves according to a Biblical standard. Madison could have easily offered the thought.

Barton's explanation contains yet additional errors. His assertion that the quotation is "consistent with Madison's thoughts on religion and government" is highly problematic. In reflecting on religion and the new Constitution, Madison thought that religion was inadequate to protect the country against the tyranny of the majority. In *Federalist 10*, Madison worried about the propensity of different factions to impose their will on the common good. Among the causes of factions he cited "a zeal for different opinions concerning religion." Further he noted that people divide into numerous religious sects and parties, parties that have "inflamed them with mutual animosity, and rendered them much more disposed to vex and oppress each other, than to co-operate for their common good." He concluded that religion was not the glue that would bind Americans together: "[W]e well know that neither moral nor religious motives can be relied on as an adequate control. They are not found to be such on the injustice and violence of individuals, and lose their efficacy in proportion to the number combined together." Thus, far from regarding religion, including Christianity, as being an adequate foundation of the new government, Madison warned against religious coalitions such as the Christian Right who claim that their brand of religion should become the foundation for a Christian America.

> (5) "Religion...[is] the basis and foundation of government."—James Madison (inaccurate).

Barton explains that this quote was "taken from Madison's *Memorial and Remonstrance* [and]...has proven to be inaccurate. The actual phrase refers to the "Declaration of those rights 'which pertain to the good people of Virginia, as the basis and foundation of Government.'" He then admits that "the subject of the statement is the *Virginia Declaration of Rights*, not religion," hardly a minor mix-up. Barton shrugs off how such an "error" could occur: "One may only speculate as to how the error was made." Given his project of rewriting history to demonstrate his ultraconservative views, one may easily speculate that the substitution of "religion" for "*Virginia Declaration of Rights*" was deliberate.

One more misquote will suffice to illustrate Barton's fabrication of evidence:

> "Whosoever shall introduce into public affairs the principles of primitive Christianity will change the face of the world."—Benjamin Franklin (unconfirmed).

Barton acknowledges that the quotation does not appear in Franklin's extensive writings. However, as he does in explaining most of the fabrications, he portrays Franklin as a person, although not a Christian, who valued the role of religion in public life. In making such a declaration, Barton confuses valuing religion with desiring a Christian nation. Franklin, like most of the founders, believed morality to be essential in a republic that rested on public virtue. Moreover, he thought the moral teachings of Jesus were sublime. Thus, without question, he thought religion, especially moral instruction, was important in the nation. Specifically, he thought elected officials should seek divine guidance. However, he did not propose that religion be the foundation of the new republic. Quite the opposite. He warned against politicians who spouted religious views in order to get votes. And he recognized that Christians could never agree on whose Christianity should prevail. At the closing of the Federal Convention he urged the delegates to put aside their biases and special interests and make the passage of the draft unanimous. In calling for agreement for the common good, he, like Madison, cited religious factionalism as a cautionary tale:

> Most men indeed as well as most sects in Religion, think themselves in possession of all truth, and that whereever

others differ from them it is so far error. Steele, a Protestant in a Dedication tells the Pope, that the only difference between our Churches in their opinions of the certainty of their doctrines is, the Church of Rome is infallible and the Church of England is never in the wrong. But though many private persons think almost as highly of their own infallibility as of that of their sect, few express it so naturally as a certain french lady, who in a dispute with her sister, said "I don't know how it happens, Sister but I meet with no body but myself, that's always in the right."

In pledging to be more careful in his research, Barton reveals his lack of understanding regarding historical investigation. He prefaced his discussion of the fabricated quotations with the following statement, which warrants being reprinted in full:

> The following quotations have been seen and heard in numerous books, periodicals, editorials, speeches, etc. In our research, we have not previously used a quote that was not documented to a source in a manner that would be acceptable in a scholarly work or a university text. However, *we strongly believe that the debates surrounding the Founders are too important to apply solely an academic standard.* [My emphasis] Therefore, we unilaterally initiated within our own works a standard of documentation that would exceed the academic standard and instead would conform to the superior legal standard (i.e., relying solely on primary or original sources, using best evidence, rather than relying on the writings of attorneys, professors, or historians).

The statement in italics begs the question of what exactly is Barton's standard if not that of the standard accepted by professional historians. He purports to be a historian, yet does not adhere to the profession's standards for historical research. His statement gives a clue as to his standard: the Christian Right's belief that the importance of the founders' testimony transcends that of accurate, documented quotations, apparently justifying fabrications.

Barton is unwilling to acknowledge his fabrications, so he shifts attention to his new, "much higher standards," by which the questionable quotations are, in his word, "unconfirmed." He fails to understand or admit that what he calls "much higher standards" are and have long been the norm for the academic historians he criticizes. Indeed, no undergraduate history major in a respectable history department would fabricate quotations as Barton has. While all historians occasionally make mistakes regarding quotations, such an egregious and sustained practice as followed by Barton would bring professional disgrace.

In addition to fabricating evidence or using "unconfirmed" quotations, Christian Right "historians" select only quotations that substantiate their claims while ignoring those that weaken or even contradict them. Their hope is to amass such a concentration of the founders' quotes on religion that no one can conclude anything other than that they were devout and committed Christians. What they fail to do is to demonstrate that the founders' expressed Christian beliefs—and without question the vast majority were professing Christians—translated into the formation of a Christian state. Consider William Federer's list of quotations from Andrew Jackson. In a tribute to Jackson on his "American Minute" series, Federer lists selective quotes, including Jackson's reflections on his wife, Rachel, uttered shortly after her death: "We cannot recall her, we are commanded by our dear Saviour, not to mourn for the dead, but for the living;" [and] "She has changed a world of woe for a world of eternal happiness, and we ought to prepare as we too must follow...'The Lord's will be done on earth as it is in heaven.'" Federer ended this segment by stating, "Of the Bible, Andrew Jackson stated,

'That book, Sir, is the Rock upon which our republic rests.'"[15] From those quotations one concludes that Jackson had a belief in Christ as Savior, in an afterlife, and in the Bible as the surest foundation for human society. But they do not indicate Jackson's views on the central issue of the relationship between church and state, and Jackson made those views clear, although Federer chose not to include those because they ran counter to his beliefs. In a letter to the Synod of the Reformed Church of North America, dated 12 June 1832, Jackson explained his refusal of their request that he proclaim a day of fasting, humiliation, and prayer: "I could not do otherwise without transcending the limits prescribed by the Constitution for the President and without feeling that I might in some degree disturb the security which religion nowadays enjoys in this country in its complete separation from the political concerns of the General Government." Here Jackson, who elsewhere expressed his personal beliefs in the Christian faith, stated his commitment to the principle of separation of church and state. Federer ignored this explicit statement, hoping that his readers would infer from Jackson's personal beliefs that he also believed in close ties between church and state. This is bad history: misleading, biased, and deceptive.

Other Christian Right "historians" misinterpret the evidence that they present through faulty logic. For instance, in his book, *Christianity and the Constitution*, John Eidsmoe claims that the United States Constitution reflects more the thought of John Calvin than that of Enlightenment thinkers like Locke and Montesquieu, as "liberals" and "secularists" claim. And, he argues that the founders themselves found inspiration from the writings of Calvin

---

[15] Quotations are found on Federer's "American Minute" postings. See http://www.crossroad.to/Quotes/american-minute.htm.

and the Bible more so than from political history, political philosophy, and political theory. Eidsmoe has been something of a crusader for what he deems to be the ignored Christian influence on the Constitution. Among his lectures are the following titles: "John Calvin: America's First Founding Father" and "Calvin's Doctrine of Interposition," an argument that it was Calvin who laid the foundations for one of Eidsmoe's favorite political hobbyhorses, states' rights. In his book, Eidsmoe hammers away at his insistence that the Constitution was built explicitly on Christian principles. That conclusion rests, however, on the logical fallacy of confusing similarity with causation. Throughout his work, he cites a principle or phrase found in the Constitution and then finds what he considers to be a similar idea in the writings of Calvin, concluding that the similarity "proves" that the founders looked to Calvin for their source of inspiration, a logical fallacy known as *post hoc ergo propter hoc* (after this, therefore, because of this).

A brief analysis of how Eidsmoe uses evidence in his book illustrates the fallacy. He opens by claiming that most Americans in the eighteenth century embraced Calvinism as the theological foundation of their faith. While that is probably accurate for active Christians, the mere presence of Calvinism does not explain whether or not it influenced the writing of the Constitution. To do that, one would have to demonstrate that the delegates to the Federal Convention in 1787 pored over Calvin's works as a source for how they should structure the new republic and what powers to grant to its constituent parts. Further, the delegates were not representative of the population as a whole. They were wealthier, better educated, more experienced in political matters, and better informed of political history and theory. When one conducts a keyword search of the surviving records of the Convention of 1787, one finds no mention of Calvin or Calvinism. On the other hand, Montesquieu is mentioned thirteen times. One would think that if the delegates were influenced by Calvin directly, they would refer to him by name or at least cite his writings as they did Montesquieu's. Eidsmoe, however, went into his study wanting to believe in the Christian foundations of the United States, and he found them despite the absence of direct evidence. For instance, he dismisses the "secularist" interpretation that the Constitution reflects John Locke's notion of the "social contract." Eidsmoe insists instead that the Constitution rests on the Puritan idea of covenant, that is, the covenant that was the foundation of Massachusetts Bay Colony's Christian commonwealth, which, in turn, was modeled after the Abrahamic covenant of the Old Testament. By conflating the Puritan and biblical notion of covenant with the Lockean idea of social contract, Eidsmoe tries to convert the Constitution from an Enlightenment-inspired document to a Christian treatise.

A comparison between the Puritan covenant of Massachusetts in 1629 and the social contract expressed in, first, the Declaration of Independence in 1776 and, second, the U.S. Constitution of 1787 illustrates the failure of Eidsmoe to account for the significant differences between Puritan covenant and social contract. In speaking for the Massachusetts Puritans, Governor John Winthrop declared that a covenant existed between the Puritans and God. Explicitly, he asserted that God had endorsed the undertaking of the Puritans to create a commonwealth based on Scripture. Like the Mosaic and Abrahamic covenants, the Puritan covenant was conditional; if the Puritans submitted to God's law and were obedient to His commandments, He would bless their endeavor, but if they turned from Him, He would withdraw his support. That covenant was the basis for the Massachusetts Puritans' claim that they were the new Chosen People, an American Israel. By contrast, the social contract of the Declaration of Independence was drawn up by the People to regulate relations between the governed and their governors. The People claimed sole authority in dictating the terms of that relationship. If their governors protected their rights, the People would submit to their government, but if they did not, the People reserved the right to remove the governors. Unlike English Crowns who claimed to rule by "divine right," governors in the new United States would rule under popular sovereignty.

The ideas of a social contract and popular sovereignty were also underscored in the Preamble to the U.S. Constitution. The contract was drawn up by the People: "We the People...." Neither God nor Church nor Christianity nor the Bible was sovereign; the Constitution was drafted in the name of and under the sole authority of the People. And the People brought the new republic into existence, not to advance the Kingdom of God or to pledge submission to God's Will or to live under the dictates of Scripture, but to attain specific secular goals: "We the people of the United States, in order to form a more perfect union, establish justice, insure domestic tranquility, provide for the common defense, promote the general welfare, and secure the blessings of liberty to ourselves and our posterity, do ordain and establish this Constitution for the United States of America."

Sound historical investigation demands that texts be scrutinized within historical context, a demand honored mainly in the breach by Christian Rights "historians." In this instance, Eidsmoe makes strained and tenuous links between Calvinist ideas and Constitutional principles, paying almost no attention to the circumstances that faced the delegates in 1787. When one considers context, one is better able to understand the concerns of the delegates and why they chose the specific aims outlined in the Preamble. The first goal reflects the delegates' recognition for a stronger central government, one that had sufficient power to correct the weaknesses of the current constitution, the Articles of Confederation. Thus, "a more perfect union" was the primary desire, one that would stop the practice of a single state from holding the Confederation hostage. Under the articles, the states alone possessed taxing authority; Congress could request new taxes, but only the states could levy them. With the continental currency severely depreciated and Congress unable to fund external threats to the national interest, Superintendent of Finance Robert Morris proposed an excise tax. Twelve states agreed to the tax, but Rhode Island opposed it, so the measure failed. Such an instance of states placing local interests above the common good prompted the calling of the Federal Convention and explains the pride of place of "a more perfect union" in the Preamble.

The other five purposes set forth in the Preamble also address immediate problems confronting the United States. While the delegates hoped that the Constitution they were drafting would endure for future generations, they were primarily concerned with issues of their day. Consider a couple more. The aim of ensuring domestic tranquility was inspired in no small part by the events surrounding Shays' Rebellion, a civil conflict that raged in Massachusetts in 1786, when some Revolutionary veterans in the western part of the state were unable to pay taxes on their farms because of the post-war recession and because of the depreciated Continental Notes with which they had been paid for their military service. The notes had fallen in value to about ten cents on the dollar in large part because the states failed to provide Congress with sufficient revenues to fund the debt. Thus, delegates to the Federal Convention desired a stronger union with independent taxing authority in order to prevent future disturbances like Shays' Rebellion.

The purpose of providing for the common defense stemmed from the many threats that the country faced from enemies nearby and abroad. Americans wishing to move West encountered hostile native groups. Settlers already in the West were unable to ship their goods down the Mississippi River because Spain closed it to American commerce. Even though Britain had recognized American independence in 1783, Britain refused to accede to American demands for a commercial treaty. Moreover, the British closed their West Indies markets to the U.S., markets that had once been America's most lucrative. And, perhaps most humiliating of all, the "petty states" (Jefferson's description) of North Africa, the so-called Barbary States— Algiers, Tripoli, and Tunis, plus the Kingdom of Morocco— began seizing American merchantmen in 1784, one year after the U.S. became independent, thereby closing the Mediterranean to American shipping. So, on all sides, the United States had its independence circumscribed, and the delegates sought a more powerful union and central government to create a military establishment sufficient to protect American interests around the world.

Despite all evidence to the contrary, Eidsmoe and the other Christian Right "historians" assert that the delegates in 1787 were fired by religious zeal and strove to create a Christian state. Moreover, they insist that the purposes stated in the Preamble were biblically inspired and thus must be regarded as sacred and not secular aims. Such narrow focus results from the fallacy of reductionism, that is, the belief that all matters, no matter how complex, can and should be reduced to a single explanation. In this case, all is reduced to religion. According to the *Oxford English Dictionary*, a reductionist is a "person who attempts to analyse or account for a complex theory or phenomenon by reduction." In doing just that, the Christian Right "historians" are guilty of the same sin they accuse academic historians of committing. They rail against those who reduce American history to economics, for example, to the exclusion of religion. When the delegates assembled in Philadelphia in 1787, the biggest issue before them was union, not religion. Most of them were satisfied that their respective state constitutions had settled religious questions, thus religion rarely emerged as a topic at the Federal Convention.

If Christian Right "historians" wish to be taken seriously as historians, they must submit their work to a rigorous vetting process similar to that followed by university presses. When an academic historian sends a manuscript to a university press, it is read quickly by one or more editors who decide if the topic and quality of scholarship fit the press's interests and standards. If so, the manuscript is forwarded to several, usually from three to five, outside readers who are published scholars of the topic and who are well acquainted with existing historiography and primary source material. These scholars read the manuscript closely for the selection and use of evidence, the organization and logic of the argument, the accuracy of quotations, and the conclusions drawn from the evidence cited. They submit reader reports to the editor recommending publication with or without revisions or recommending that the press does not publish the manuscript. After making revisions, the author resubmits the manuscript (a process that might be repeated) for text editing and publication. Then after publication, the book is reviewed by scholars who again comment on the quality of the scholarship as well as the book's arguments and major conclusions. Such a vetting process does not guarantee that all works published by academic historians are without flaws, but it does mean that those flaws are likely to be found and made public. Moreover, the body of works published by academic historians on a particular topic, say the American Revolution or the U.S. Constitution, represents sound scholarship that invites additional commentary and criticism. By contrast, much of material published by the Christian Right "historians" is either self-published or published by presses devoted to their particular causes. For example, David Barton publishes his ideas primarily on his website, WallBuilders, which means that his works are largely self-published, meaning that he writes, edits, and publishes his own materials. Ironically, one of the founders that he likes to quote (or misquote), James Madison, noted in *Federalist 10* that "[n]o man is allowed to be a judge in his own cause, because his interest would certainly bias his judgment, and, not improbably, corrupt his integrity." While Madison was arguing that legislators should not be allowed to judge the constitutionality of their own acts, the sentiment applies to authors as well.

Christian Right "Historians" and Partisan Politics

The "histories" fabricated by the Christian Right have contributed to the politicization of religion in America that has accelerated since the 1970s when Presidential candidates began making their personal religion an integral part of their campaigns. Prior to then, candidates rarely mentioned their religious beliefs unless the opposition made them a campaign issue. Such was the case in 1800 when a group of New England clergymen who supported

John Adams charged Thomas Jefferson with being an atheist. Jefferson's supporters countered by suggesting that Adams wished to introduce a Presbyterian establishment. Both charges were inaccurate, and both proceeded from highly partisan motives. Jefferson won the election and Adams thought the issue of religion was decisive, although the absence of exit polls made such pronouncements on voter motivation problematic. Then in the 1928 and 1960 Presidential campaigns, Catholic nominees of the Democratic Party came under withering attacks for their religious beliefs; Al Smith lost in 1928, and John Kennedy won in 1960, although neither outcome can be attributed solely to religion. In all other campaigns, candidates regarded their religious views as personal and by and large they kept them private. Perhaps Harry Truman spoke for most candidates when as a young man he expressed his views about making public declarations of one's religious beliefs: "I am by religion as I am like everything else, I think there is more in acting than in talking. I had an uncle who said when one of his neighbors got religion strong on Sunday, he was going to lock his smokehouse on Monday."[16] It was Jimmy Carter, the Democratic hopeful in the 1976 race, who made his personal religion a centerpiece of his campaign. Appealing to white Southern evangelicals who had defected from the Democratic Party *en masse* following the passage of the Civil Rights Act of 1964 and the Voting Rights Act of 1965, Carter repeatedly referred to his Southern Baptist faith and publicly professed to be a

---

[16] Quotation taken from "Harry Truman Speaks," compiled by Raymond Geselbracht and posted on the Truman Presidential Museum and Library website: http://www.trumanlibrary.org/speaks.html (accessed 11 June 2007).

"born-again" Christian. He was frequently photographed entering or exiting a church with his Bible in his hand.

Then in the 1980 campaign, Republican candidate Ronald Reagan, with the backing of the Christian Right, defeated Carter. A Christian Right "historian" played no small role. As discussed earlier, it was Tim LaHaye who pronounced that Carter's "liberal" views on the family meant that the President's administration was "un-Christian." Ironically, LaHaye endorsed the divorced Reagan as the champion who would fight for "family values."

Newt Gingrich is another "historian" of the Christian Right who has continued the Conservative crusade to beatify and canonize Reagan as a stalwart Christian President. The past created by Gingrich is particularly egregious because he has a Ph.D. in history from Tulane University and knows full well that a fair and thorough examination of the founding era within historical context presents unwelcome conclusions for all partisan politicians. But he is a partisan politician, a self-avowed Ronald Reagan Conservative. So he ignores the tenets of good history and goes for the usable past. One example will suffice. He wrote the foreword to a book titled *The New Reagan Revolution: How Ronald Reagan's Principles Can Restore American Greatness* (2011), which links present-day Conservatives with the nation's founders. In that work, the authors, Michael Reagan and Jim Denney, write, "[W]e conservatives believe (as the Founding Fathers did) in far more freedom and far less government." And, in good partisan strategy, they set up a stark contrast with their political opponents: "Liberals see the Constitution as malleable and elastic. Conservatives believe the Constitution should be interpreted in terms of the original intent of its framers." A cursory exploration of the debates at the Constitutional Convention, the state Ratifying

Conventions, and the first Washington administration reveals that the founders were divided over that same question and that many who saw themselves as "liberal and enlightened" favored a malleable Constitution that would fit changing circumstances. But, the authors, with Gringich's endorsement, take the partisan road: "Ronald Reagan's principles are those of the Founding Fathers," as if the original founders were of one mind and as if those who disagree with Reagan are unprincipled.[17] Moreover, the authors make much about the original founders' faith in God, thus setting up the lineage of God, the founding fathers, Ronald Reagan, and Conservative Republicans. So a vote for Conservative Republicans is an endorsement of Ronald Reagan, an affirmation of the principles of the founding fathers, and a confession of faith in God. With that usable past firmly established as the "real" history of the founding, those who oppose Conservative Republicans are then opponents of the Reagan Revolution, violators of the principles of the founding fathers, and godless or at least deniers of God's place in the lineage according to Gingrich and the authors.

Gingrich was one of four candidates seeking the Republican nomination for the Presidency in 2012 who made their religion a major part of their campaigns. And they larded their partisan talk with religious language. Michelle Bachmann graduated from the Oral Roberts School of Law where she studied under John Eidsmoe. The ORU Law School touts itself as "interdenominational, Bible-based, and Holy Spirit-led." In an April campaign speech, Bachmann said of her choice to attend ORU: "My goal there

---

[17] See Michael Reagan and Jim Denney, *The New Reagan Revolution: How Ronald Reagan's Principles Can Restore American Greatness* (New York: Thomas Dunne Books, 2011).

was to learn the law both from a professional but also from a biblical worldview."[18] Throughout her campaign, she emphasized her "faith-based" view of politics, linking her faith with Conservative Tea Party political ideas. During the campaign, she lauded "the Founding Fathers" and derided those who in any way criticized them. On one occasion, she declared that the founders "worked hard" to eliminate slavery, an astounding view considering that some of the most notable founders, including Washington and Jefferson and Madison, were slaveholders who profited from the labor of bondsmen. She later cited John Adams's son, John Quincy Adams, as one who spoke against slavery.

As Bachmann's candidacy stalled in the early primaries, the Christian Right rallied behind Texas Governor William Perry. At a kickoff rally in Texas, Christian Right leaders hoped that the Conservative governor would challenge frontrunner Mitt Romney, whose Mormon faith made him suspect, if not outright unacceptable, to the Right. Perry pledged to return America to God, who, as RightWingWatch quoted, had "sent storms to keep him in Texas and was using the economic crisis to 'bring us back to those biblical principles.'" Leaders from the Christian Right lined up behind Perry. Pat Robertson declared that Perry "founded his administration on the Bible."[19] Jerry Falwell, Jr., viewed him as the second coming of Ronald Reagan.

When Perry's campaign faltered, Newt Gingrich stepped in. He, too, made religion a central piece of his campaign with the publication of *God in America* (2007), a

---

[18] Cited in Jonathan Chait, "Michelle Bachmann's Intellectual Worldview," *The New Republic*, 15 June 2011.

[19] Quoted on the Perry supporters' website, People for the American Way: http://www.pfaw.org/category/people/rick-perry (accessed 12 July 2012).

book written with his wife, Callista, which offers a "walking tour" through American history showing how religion has been prominent in shaping America's founding and the nation's institutions. Like David Barton, Gingrich's view of history is restorationist, that is, an attempt to "rediscover" religious symbols that "radical secularists" wish to remove from the public square. As a candidate, Gingrich positioned himself as "the" Conservative choice and cast himself as a Conservative Christian, a recent convert to the Catholic Church. But, alas, his campaign was lackluster, and he, too, gained no ground on Romney.

Rick Santorum was the Republican candidate who most blatantly politicized religion in his campaign. A staunch Catholic, Santorum reiterated an earlier claim that "Satan has his sights on the U.S." because it has turned away from its Christian heritage. While stating that he "accepts the fact that the president is a Christian," Santorum declared that Obama's faith rested on some "phony theology."[20] By contrast, Santorum paraded his Christianity as the right theology, suggesting that those who disagreed with his ultraconservative views were wrong or "phony." But, despite enjoying considerable support from the Christian Right, Santorum succumbed to the Romney juggernaut.

Thus, in the end, the Republican hopefuls who made their religious views central to their campaigns lost. Why they lost cannot be explained simply because of their politicization of religion, but it could have been a contributing factor. Americans cherish religious liberty and resent anyone, including, or especially, political candidates, telling them what beliefs or morals to embrace. In the end,

---

[20] See "Rick Santorum Says He Was Not Questioning Obama's Faith with 'Phony Theology' Remark," *Washington Post*, 19 February 2012.

the one candidate whose religious identity was under constant attack from the Christian Right prevailed. Then, in supreme irony, Christian Right leaders who assailed Romney's Mormonism as a non-Christian "cult" began to rally behind his candidacy against Obama only if Romney left his religion out of his administration. Pat Robertson stated his hope and belief that Romney would not "interject the Mormon religion into the way he governs."[21] In other words, Romney was acceptable only if he was entirely secular. While railing against secularists for so long, the Christian Right, including such high-profile figures as Billy and Franklin Graham, now welcomed the Republican candidate if he dropped all hints of his religious faith and adopted a purely secular course. For them, even a secular Republican was preferable to Obama and his liberal policies. Such a stance suggests that the fine line between the Christian Right's religious and political orientation was erased in favor of Conservative politics.

After securing his party's nomination and turning his attention to the general election in November, Romney spoke out on religion. In August, Romney and the Republican National Committee aired an ad titled, "Be Not Afraid." While he did not mention his Mormon faith, Romney questioned Obama, declaring that the President has waged a "war on religion," citing provisions in Obama's healthcare initiative that requires employers, including the Catholic Church, to provide contraceptive devices if the employer offers medical insurance as a benefit. Further, the ad featured quotes and images of Pope John Paul II as a way of identifying with a popular

---

[21] See "Pat Robertson: Vote Romney Because 'You Don't Have Jesus Running,'" posted on 14 May 2012 at http://www.rawstory.com/rs/2012/05/14/pat-robertson-vote-romney-because-you-dont-have-jesus-running/ (accessed 10 August 2012).

Christian leader.[22] While critics saw the ad as another example of politicizing religion, Romney and the Republicans hoped to shore up the candidate's Christian leanings while excoriating the President as anti-religious.

There are signs that the Christian Right and their "historians" are losing support even among those who consider themselves Conservatives. Two who have voiced criticism are Cal Thomas, Conservative newspaper columnist and early supporter of the Moral Majority, and Ed Dobson, onetime assistant to Jerry Falwell and pastor of a megachurch in Grand Rapids, Michigan. In their book, *Blinded by Might* (1999), they declare the Moral Majority a failure as a political force. Dobson points out that despite all of the bombast and hubris expressed through the most vocal Christian Right rhetoric, there is little indication that that rhetoric has stemmed the tide of crime, pornography, homosexuality, and abortion: "[E]very plank of our [Moral Majority] platform we have failed from a legislative and judicial perspective." Thomas thought it time for the Christian Right to "admit that because we are using the wrong weapons, we are losing the fight." While he and Dobson did not abandon Conservative moral positions, they did call for a shift in tactics, one that would unfold in churches and homes and communities, not in political halls of power. They called for Christians to change American culture by being obedient to biblical tenets, rather than engaging in electoral politics. They might have added that by politicizing religion, the Christian Rightists lost their prophetic voice and became just another partisan group clamoring for its pet causes. Moreover, they charged that by

---

[22] See "Romney Accuses Obama of 'War on Religion,'" posted on 9 August 2012 by *America: The National Catholic Weekly* on its website: http://www.americamagazine.org/blog/entry.cfm?blog_id=2&entry_id= 5287 (accessed 10 August 2012).

making politics their tactic, the Christian Right had promoted Christian arrogance rather than moral reformation. Perhaps their most telling indictment came as Thomas and Dobson rejected one of the central claims of Christian Right "historians": that America was conceived of and is a Christian nation. Thomas asserted that the Christian Right "set America apart and above all other nations. This is heresy."[23]

Liberals have long criticized the Christian Right and their "historians" for their anti-intellectualism, but recently some Conservatives have agreed. In a 17 October 2011 *New York Times* op-ed piece titled, "The Evangelical Rejection of Reason," Karl W. Giberson, a former professor of physics, and Randall J. Stephens, an associate professor of history, both at Eastern Nazarene College, concluded from comments made by Conservative Republican Presidential hopefuls and their evangelical backers that "[t]he Republican presidential field has become a showcase of evangelical anti-intellectualism." They wrote, "Herman Cain, Rick Perry, and Michele Bachmann deny that climate change is real and caused by humans. Mr. Perry and Mrs. Bachmann dismiss evolution as an unproven theory. The two candidates who espouse the greatest support for science, Mitt Romney and Jon M. Huntsman, Jr., happen to be Mormons, a faith regarded with mistrust by many Christians." The writers identified themselves as accepting "the centrality of faith in Jesus Christ and look to the Bible as our sacred book," but they found the Fundamentalism of the Christian Right to be "literalistic, overconfident, and reactionary." They accused spokespersons for the Right of denying almost everything coming from the academy,

---

[23] Cited in Frank Lambert *Religion in American Politics: A Short History* (Princeton: Princeton University Press, 2008), 212.

whether the history of academic historians or the science of academic scientists. Instead, they charged that some of the most Conservative "evangelicals created what amounts to a 'parallel culture,' nurtured by church, Sunday school, summer camps, and colleges, as well as publishing houses, broadcasting networks, music festivals, and counseling groups." They identified David Barton as one of the chief "orchestrators—and beneficiaries—of this subculture." Through repeated assertion, selective evidence, and specious reasoning, Barton and his colleagues dismiss scholarship and appeal to their readers' preconceptions and biases to accept their claims.[24]

Despite their attacks on anyone who disagrees with them, Christian Right "historians" frequently take on the mantle of victims for their causes. They interpret any attack on their particular brand of Christianity as an attack on religion itself. In fact, most of those who oppose the Christian Right are not "radical secularists," but Christians who object to Fundamentalist and intolerant views that are represented by the Right as the legacies of America's religious heritage. Opponents are not saying, "We oppose religion, in general, or Christianity in particular"; rather, they are saying, "We oppose *your* brand of religion and object to your attempt to impose it on the nation."

Undeterred, Christian Right zealots, like those on the Texas School Board, are determined to rewrite American history to conform to their religious views. Their primary assertion is that America was founded as a Christian state, but curiously they avoid close scrutiny of the one example

---

[24] Karl Giberson and Randall Stephens, "The Evangelical Rejection of Reason," published as an op-ed piece in the *New York Times*, 17 October 2011.

of a Christian commonwealth in America's past, that of the
Puritan colony of Massachusetts Bay Colony.

Massachusetts Bay Colony:
Early American Model of a Christian Nation

When William Williams first read the draft constitution for the United States in late 1787, he was surprised and disappointed. The merchant and delegate to the Connecticut Ratifying Convention descended from Puritans, and he had wanted and expected a preamble fitting for a Christian nation, one closer to that his Puritan forefathers had espoused. Williams was appalled that there was no acknowledgment of God's Providence, nor any mention of God at all in the Preamble. While there were six purposes stated for the newly constituted government, not one was to further the Kingdom of God. He, therefore, proposed a new Preamble that read in part: "We the people of the United States, in a firm belief of the being and perfections of the one living and true God, the creator and supreme Governour of the world, in his universal providence and the authority of his laws; that he will require of all moral agents an account of their conduct; that all rightful powers among men are ordained of, and mediately derived from God."[1] Williams's suggestion went

---

[1] Philip Kurland and Ralph Lerner, eds., *The Founders' Constitution*, 4 vols. (Chicago: University of Chicago Press, 1987) 4:643.

unheeded, and the Constitution was ratified without any change to the Preamble.

Unlike Williams, Isaac Backus of Massachusetts was delighted with the Constitution's treatment of religion. A dissenter and itinerant Baptist preacher, Backus and his family had experienced firsthand religious persecution under the colony's establishment laws. In 1752, Backus's mother was jailed for refusing to pay taxes to support the establishment, which required all citizens to contribute to the Congregational Churches. And, because of his itinerant preaching in Connecticut, Isaac faced a hostile legislature that imposed fines on unlicensed preachers. Thus, as a delegate to the Massachusetts ratifying convention, Backus was delighted to see that Congress had no grant of power whatever over religion and that all religious tests were prohibited. He saw all such tests as engines of tyranny and the absence of them as protection against any religious establishment. He wrote, "Some serious minds discover a concern lest, if all *religious tests* should be excluded, that Congress would hereafter establish Popery, or some other tyrannical way of worship. But it is most certain that no such way of worship can be established without any *religious test.*"[2]

Williams's and Backus's contrasting views of the Constitution were based on their divergent interpretations of the Puritan commonwealths established in New England in the seventeenth century. Williams thought the Christian states erected there promoted religious orthodoxy and moral rectitude, and he, therefore, recalled them in a positive light. Backus saw them through the eyes of a dissenter and believed that their insistence on religious

---

[2] Jonathan Elliott, ed., *The Debates in the Several State Conventions on the Adoption of the Federal Constitution*, 5 vols. (Philadelphia, 1888) 2:148–49.

uniformity violated the sacred individual right of liberty of conscience. Williams saw the Holy Commonwealths of Connecticut and Massachusetts as models worthy of emulation in the new republic; Backus regarded them as something to be avoided.

An examination of Puritan New England, and particularly the Christian commonwealth of Massachusetts, enables us to understand what the two men favored and feared, respectively. It also allows us to explore life in a Christian state that actually existed. Christian Right "historians" conflate English settlement of North America in the early seventeenth century with the establishment of the republic in the late eighteenth century. The result distorts history and undermines their argument that the U.S. was founded as a Christian state. As this chapter reveals, Puritans did indeed establish Christian states, but delegates to the Federal Convention of 1787 chose to ignore them in favor of a secular frame of government.

Massachusetts Bay and Connecticut were constituted explicitly as Christian colonies. Both exhibited everything that the Christian Right "historians" claim for the United States. They were established by devout Christians for Christian purposes and based their constitutions and laws on biblical principles. While the evidence in the following chapters challenges the assertion of the United States conceived of as a Christian state, without question Connecticut and Massachusetts Bay Colony are shining examples of Christian commonwealths. They, therefore, offer an opportunity to examine what a Christian state looks like: its purposes, institutions, and mission. The founders of Massachusetts Bay Colony formed what the Christian Right claim they want to see in America today: a Christian society based on biblical laws under a government of Christian leaders. But their strict enforcement of religious uniformity restricted individual freedom, and thus violated other sacred principles of the Christian Right, such as free enterprise unfettered by government regulation. While Christian Right "historians" cite the Puritan colonies in New England as evidence of America's Christian heritage, they avoid the close analysis that reveals a state that undermined what Americans regard as sacred rights and freedom.

Christian Right "historians" presuppose that the United States was born as a Christian nation in a general sense, that is, not as the establishment of a particular expression of Christianity but as the establishment of Christianity in general. However, all historical examples of Christian establishments favor a particular branch or interpretation of Christianity. That was the case at the time of the English colonization of North America. England was considered to be a Protestant nation but was defined more precisely by its establishment: the Church of England. Indeed, Puritans left England because they were dissatisfied with the Church of England, charging that it did not adhere to basic biblical principles. England's rival, Spain, was also a Christian nation, but of course its particular establishment was that of the Catholic Church. There is no historical example of a Christian nation that conformed to beliefs and practices that all Christians could embrace. Even if based on the Bible, any Christian nation rests on some sect's interpretation. Such was the case of Massachusetts Bay Colony. While purporting to be a Christian commonwealth, it was in fact a Puritan commonwealth.

An examination of Massachusetts Bay Colony enables us to move from the consideration of a Christian nation in the abstract to that of a historical example, and it allows us to see how that particular example squares with the values and principles espoused by the Christian Right.

Massachusetts offered much that Fundamentalists from the Christian Right would admire, but it also represented much that radical right-wing Republicans would find repugnant.

An American Example of a "Christian State": The "City upon the Hill" Revisited

Americans have two sets of founders: the "planting fathers," who planted colonies in North America, and the "founding fathers," who declared and fought for independence and established a new republic. Sometimes Americans conflate these founders, treating them as a single group that created what became the United States. The Christian Right "historians" often ascribe to the "founding fathers'" beliefs and actions that more accurately belong to the "planting fathers." For instance, John Eidsmoe contends that the delegates to the Federal Convention in 1787 were guided by the Puritan concept of covenant. While he is correct in recognizing the idea of compact or covenant in the nation's founding documents, he misreads the Puritan notion of covenant with that found in the Declaration of Independence and the U.S. Constitution. The Puritan covenant was ordered on the Old Testament model of God's covenant with Moses and Abraham: God drew up the covenant and set the conditions. It was God who agreed to make the people of Israel (and in the seventeenth century, the people of Massachusetts Bay) His chosen people and grant them favor as long as they were obedient and kept His commandments. By contrast, the social compact of the U.S. founding documents was drawn up by "the people" to regulate affairs between them and their governors. The governed pledged to live under the rule of their governors only as long as they safeguarded the rights of the people.

William Williams recognized the difference. He wanted a new republic that looked like the old Puritan commonwealths of Connecticut and Massachusetts. He lamented the absence of explicit language that announced to the world that the United States was conceived of as a Christian nation, was instituted under Christian laws, and served a Christian purpose. To him, the "founding fathers" had fallen short of what the "planting fathers" had established.

Like Williams, many Conservative Christians today call for closer ties between church and state. They argue that the country was once a "Christian State," but in post-World War II America, "liberals" and "secularists" have tried to remove religion from the public stage. They argue that delegates to the Federal Convention of 1787 founded the United States as a Christian state, that is, a state built by Christian men on Christian principles. While they are correct in pointing out that virtually all of the delegates were professing Christians, they are unconvincing in claiming that the delegates built a republic on Christian principles. Delegates consulted Montesquieu, not Calvin, on how to structure power. And, while the exact phrase "separation of church and state" does not appear in the Constitution, the principle of separation is central to the document. Power is separated between the federal and state governments (although the phrase "states' rights" does not appear), and power is separated between the three branches of government (although the phrase "separation of powers" is absent). Fearing state intrusion on liberty of conscience, the delegates made no grant of power whatsoever to the federal government regarding religion. And fearing church intrusion on civil rights, the delegates made qualifications for officeholding independent of one's religious affiliation. Thus, religion was left in the hands of individuals and the states, free to thrive in a free marketplace of religion where the support of religion was voluntary.

Conservative Christians would be on much more solid ground in pointing to Massachusetts Bay Colony as a Christian state. Founded in 1629 by Puritans fleeing religious persecution in England, the colony was explicitly established as a Christian or Holy or Bible commonwealth. Governor John Winthrop laid out his vision in his sermon, "A Model of Christian Charity." Central to his view was his claim that the Puritans were in covenant with God and, as a New Israel, would enjoy God's favor as long as they submitted to His will. Biblical principles would undergird every aspect of the society—social, cultural, political, and economic—and if the people adhered to those principles, Massachusetts Bay would become a beacon to Protestants everywhere: an exemplary city upon a hill.

Church and state had separate but complementary roles in Massachusetts Bay. The church alone decided doctrine, but the state punished heretics who offended doctrinal purity. Religious uniformity was a central organizing principle, one that defined religious freedom as freedom from error. That is, a people following God's Word should be rid of all dissenters, and the government enforced that view. Bounded freedom set the parameters for all human endeavors in the colony. Merchants were free to trade but were compelled to adhere to biblical laws of a "fair price" and a "just wage." And, the state enforced those restrictions. Citizens were free to hold office only if they had proven themselves as "visible saints," that is, as members in good standing of a congregation. And, once again, the state accepted the church's role as the nominating agency for civil officeholding.

Revisiting the Christian state of Massachusetts Bay affords one a glimpse of life under a Christian regime and offers caution to those seeking closer church-state ties. While phrases like "city upon a hill" may inspire a people to strive for a society built explicitly on God's Word, one must look beyond the vision to examine how the colony in fact functioned. We know that the Holy Commonwealth officially ceased to exist when Charles II revoked the colony's charter in 1684, but it was under great internal strain long before then as individuals pushed the limits of bounded freedom and dissented against magistrates and ministers who enforced uniformity. In revisiting the city upon a hill, one encounters what many Puritan ministers called declining religious fervor, but one also sees a clash between individuals' quest for freedom and society's insistence on order.

Massachusetts Bay Colony was, according to its early settlers and subsequent generations, founded as a Christian colony. It occupied a unique position among the thirteen colonies that the English planted on North American soil. While religion was a factor in founding the other twelve, it was *the* reason for settling Massachusetts. Cotton Mather discussed motivations in his *Magnalia Christi Americana*, written in the early eighteenth century to explain why John Winthrop and other Puritans departed England for New England. Mather cited one of the company's investors, a Captain Weymouth, who wrote that "one main end of all these undertakings, [i.e., all the colonies] was to plant the gospel in these dark regions of America." Mather then offered his own interpretation that the settlement of Massachusetts was exceptional. "I am now to tell mankind," he wrote, "that as for one of these English plantations, this was not only a *main end*, but the *sole end* upon which it was erected." While the settlers there, like elsewhere, sought profits as well as piety, Massachusetts was "the spot of earth, which the God of heaven *spied out* for the seat of such *evangelical* and *ecclesiastical*, and very remarkable transactions." It was a place, Mather concluded, "that our blessed Jesus intended a *resting place.*"[3]

When the *Arbella* sailed into Salem harbor on 12 June 1630, she brought a company of people with a covenant from God and a divine mission. The Puritans who had fled persecution in England under Archbishop William Laud considered themselves to be nothing less than a chosen people who were determined to plant a new Israel on American soil. In a sermon delivered aboard the ship before making landfall, their governor, John Winthrop, declared that they were no ordinary people; rather, he reminded them, Scripture "teacheth us to put a difference between Christians and others." Therefore, the New England Puritans must acknowledge that they were a "Company professing [to be] fellow members of Christ," and that they must organize a new society "knit together by this bond of love." To remain pure, they must see that their communities were free from all who were outside the Gospel covenant. Thus, in the words of historian Kenneth Lockridge, the Puritans had a mission to establish "closed, Christian, corporate, utopian communities."

The bond that created the Christian commonwealth of Massachusetts was not the company's charter granted by Charles I in 1629; rather, it was a divine covenant between God and the Puritan settlers. In his sermon, *A Model of Christian Charity*, Winthrop set forth the circumstances and conditions of the covenant. He asserted that "[w]e are entered into covenant with Him for this work," adding,

---

[3] The opening of this chapter is adopted from my book, *The Founding Fathers and the Place of Religion in America* (Princeton: Princeton University Press, 2003) 73–81. For Mather's quote, see Cotton Mather, *Magnalia Christi Americana; or, The Ecclesiastical History of New England*, 2 vols. (1702; repr., Hartford: Thomas Robbins, 1853) 1:45.

"The Lord hath given us leave to draw our own articles." He explained that the Puritans had sought God's blessings on their enterprise and that God had endorsed the Puritans' undertaking in Massachusetts. However, the covenant was conditional:

> Now if the Lord shall please to hear us, and bring us in peace to the place we desire, then hath He ratified this covenant and sealed our commission, and will expect a strict performance of the articles contained in it; but if we shall neglect the observation of these articles which are the ends we have propounded, and, dissembling with our God, shall fall to embrace this present world and prosecute our carnal intentions, seeking great things for ourselves and our posterity, the Lord will surely break out in wrath against us, and be revenged of such a people, and make us know the price of the breach of such a covenant.[4]

The Cambridge Platform of 1648 represents the high-water mark of New England Puritanism, that is, the fullest expression of the Christian commonwealth. It codified how the church should be organized and governed, and it set forth relations between church and state. The prescribed form of church government set forth therein was not deemed to be one among many ways of gathering a congregation for the worship of God, but it was declared to be the "One, Immutable, and Prescribed in the Word." As in every aspect of Massachusetts life, "the Word," or Scripture, was the sole authority. Thus, "Ecclesiastical polity, or church government or discipline, is nothing else but that form and order that is to be observed in the church of Christ upon earth, both for the constitution of it, and all the administrations that therein are to be performed." The

---

[4] John Winthrop, *A Model of Christian Charity*, in [Massachusetts Historical Society] *Winthrop Papers*, 5 vols. (Boston: Mass. Hist. Soc., 1931) 2:284, 293.

Puritans' lineage was clear; they stood in the line of Moses and the Chosen People of God and in that of Christ, the head of the Church. To be true to that heritage, the Puritans must follow a government as "prescribed in the Word, because the Lord Jesus Christ, the King and Law-giver in his church, is no less faithful in the house of God, than was Moses, who from the Lord delivered a form and pattern of government to the children of Israel in the Old Testament."[5]

Individual congregations were gathered under the prescriptions set forth by the Cambridge Platform. Members were called "saints," a designation that included those who "not only attained the knowledge of the principles of religion, and are free from gross and open scandals, but also do, together with the profession of their faith and repentance, walk in blameless obedience to the Word." Membership, then, was more than pious knowledge and behavior, but a personal profession of faith in Christ and submission to His Word. Equally important, the congregation of saints must be kept pure, and those who do not profess faith in Christ and submit to his guidance must be prohibited from contaminating the saints. According to the Cambridge Platform, churches have been and should be "reproved for receiving, and suffering such persons to continue in fellowship among them, as have been offensive and scandalous; the name of God also, by this means, is blasphemed, and the holy things of God defiled and profaned, the hearts of the godly grieved, and the wicked themselves hardened and helped forward to damnation."

---

[5] For all references to the Cambridge Platform, see: *A Platform of Church Discipline Gathered out of the Word of God: and Agreed upon by the Elders: and Messengers of the Churches Assembled in the Synod at Cambridge in New England to Be Presented at the Churches and General Court for Their Consideration and Acceptance, in the Lord* (Cambridge MA: Cambridge Synod (1646-1648).

Puritans must be ever-vigilant because "the example of such does endanger the sanctity of others, a little leaven leavens the whole lump."[6]

The Christian commonwealth of Massachusetts was not meant for everyone, not even for all Protestants. It goes without saying that Catholics were not welcome, but neither were other Protestants welcomed, including Anglicans. To Puritans, intolerance of religious error was not just defensible, it was virtuous for a covenanted people to defend the purity of their faith. The settlers of Massachusetts defined religious freedom as freedom from error. To them, allowing dissenters in their midst was an act of licentiousness, not freedom. Rather than tolerating Protestants who differed from them, Puritans persecuted dissenters just as they had been persecuted in England where the Church of England was the official church. Queen Elizabeth I had recognized liberty of conscience, which meant that those critical of the Church of England could pursue their own faith so long as they did so in private. In public, there was to be no criticism of the established religion.

The Cambridge Platform declared that the state had an active role to play in maintaining the purity of the churches. It states, "It is the duty of the magistrate to take care of matters of religion, and to improve his civil authority for the observing of the duties commanded in the first, as well as for observing of the duties commanded in the second table." References to the "first" and "second table" refer to the Ten Commandments, and whereas the United States Constitution is not based on the Mosaic Law, that of Massachusetts Bay was. Civil officials were charged with maintaining the purity and righteousness of the society:

---

[6] Ibid.

"The end of the magistrate's office is not only the quiet and peaceable life of the subject in matters of righteousness and honesty, but also in matters of godliness; yea, of all godliness." Again the model for the state's role in religious matters was the Old Testament. "Moses, Joshua, David, Solomon, Asa, Jehoshaphat, Hezekiah, [and] Josiah" are cited by the platform as being "much commended by the Holy Ghost, for the putting forth their authority [sic] in matters of religion."[7]

The platform spelled out what was and what was not the jurisdiction of the civil authority. The central dividing line was that between inward belief and outward behavior: "The objects of the power of the magistrate are not things merely inward, and so not subject to his cognizance and view; as unbelief, hardness of heart, erroneous opinions not vented, but only such things as are acted by the outward man." Therefore, "[i]dolatry, blasphemy, heresy, venting corrupt and pernicious opinions, that destroy the foundation, open contempt of the Word preached, profanation of the Lord's Day, disturbing the peaceable administration and exercise of the worship and holy things of God, and the like, are to be restrained and punished by civil authority." For the most part, churches were left to govern themselves, with no interference from the state. However, if an individual congregation caused division and dissent within the society, the state had an obligation to step in and deal with the schism. The Cambridge Platform authorized the state to intervene when a church became schismatical or corrupt: "If any church, one or more, shall grow schismatical, rending itself from the communion of other churches, or shall walk incorrigibly and obstinately in any corrupt way of their own, contrary to the rule of the

---

[7] Ibid.

Word; in such case, the magistrate is to put forth his coercive power, as the matter shall require."[8]

In Massachusetts non-Puritans were "warned out" of Puritan communities. That is, they were given to a time certain to remove themselves from the premises, a practice that drew criticism from some in England, including some Puritans. About the same time the Cambridge Platform was drafted, Nathaniel Ward, pastor at Aggawam, wrote a strong apology of Massachusetts's uniformity laws. He took issue with "unfriendly reports" that were circulating in England about Puritan intolerance in New England. He repeated some of the reports: "Wee have beene reputed a Collunies of wild Opinionists, swarmed into a remote wilder-nes to find elbow-roome for our phanatick Doctrines and practises: I trust our diligence past, and constant sedulity against such persons and courses, will plead better things for us." Ward then explained that the Puritans of Massachusetts did no more than what all good Christians should do and that is to keep their faith pure by getting rid of any corrupting influence. "I dare take upon me," he wrote, "to bee the Herauld of New-England so farre, as to proclaime to the world, in the name of our Colony, that all Familists, Antinomians, Anabaptists, and other Enthusiasts shall have free Liberty to keepe away from us, and such as will come to be gone as fast as they can, the sooner the better." Ward viewed New England as a battleground between the forces of good and evil, and he had no doubt who was behind the planting of religious errors. "If the devill might have his free option, I beleeve he would ask nothing else, but liberty to enfranchize all false Religions, and to embondage the true." Ward warned against the state's establishing acts of religious toleration as means of

---

[8] Ibid.

encouraging people to immigrate to Massachusetts. Indeed, he thought such "toleration" to be the Devil's "next subtle Stratagem he will spread to distate the Truth of God and supplant the peace of the Churches." There was a place for toleration, but Puritans must ensure that "[t]olerations in things tolerable, [are] ex-quisitely drawn out by the lines of the Scripture." Only then would they be "the sacred favours of Truth."[9]

Like intolerant Puritans, the most extreme spokesmen for the Christian Right show little tolerance for the views of Christians who oppose them in the political arena. Whether it is Tim LeHaye's questioning President Carter's Christianity because of his views of the family or David Barton's calling President Obama "America's Most Biblically-Hostile U. S. President," they claim to possess the standard of "true Christianity" by which to judge others. Seventeenth-century Puritans came under attack for their intolerance. Captain John Smith of Virginia found the Massachusetts Puritans to be hypocrites: "more precise than needs" in claiming to preach the truth while at the same time not "so good as they should be" in their behavior.[10] The Christian Right should not be surprised when their views and actions come under similar attack.

Dissent in the Christian Commonwealth

In Massachusetts Bay Colony, those who could not or would not conform to the strictures of religious uniformity were labeled dissenters. Today, because of the Constitution's separation of church and state and the absence of

---

[9] Nathaniel Ward, *The Simple Cobler of Aggawam in America*, ed. P.M. Zall (Lincoln NE: University of Nebraska, 1969) 6.

[10] Karen Kupperman, *Captain John Smith: A Select Edition of His Writings* (Chapel Hill: University of North Carolina, 1988) 270–71.

an official religion, there are no dissenters in the United States. Yet the Christian Right attacks liberals, including Christian liberals, as dissenters or opponents of America's religious heritage. However, throughout American history, such attacks have always been met with a fierce defense of individual liberty. Such was the case in the Christian commonwealth of Massachusetts Bay.

Almost from the beginning cracks appeared in the Christian commonwealth. The problem was that certain individuals dared to think for themselves and gave voice to ideas that challenged the prevailing orthodoxy. In part the issue was Protestantism itself. The Protestant Reformation struck at the very foundation of Church authority by endorsing the idea of the priesthood of the believer, which meant that there is no mediator between God and humankind in matters of salvation. Protestants held that Scripture alone was sufficient to provide the way to salvation, and that faith alone was sufficient to obtain salvation. Moreover, laypeople were encouraged to read the Bible in their own language, which meant that there were bound to be differences of interpretation. Instead of a single, unified Reformation, there were multiple expressions: Lutheran, Reformed or Calvinist, Zwinglian, and Anglican. Therefore, when the ministers and magistrates of Massachusetts Bay sought to erect walls to keep out unorthodox and impure teachings, they were bound to fail. In fact, the first heresies came from within the commonwealth itself.

Dissent in Massachusetts Bay Colony challenged every aspect of life in the Christian commonwealth, religious, economic, and political. In each instance, dissenters protested what they considered to be the stifling of individual freedom by a rigid religious uniformity. Christian Right activists champion the cause of America as a Christian nation. David Barton is on a mission to educate Americans about "the Godly foundation of our country," to promote "public policies which reflect Biblical values," and recruit Christians for the Republican Party. Like the architects of Massachusetts's Christian commonwealth, Barton has a particular vision for Christian America, that is, one based on biblical principles of his choosing and public policies that he favors. While such a country would satisfy Barton and people who believe as he does, it would be a stifling environment for dissenters. Although his "history" of America refers to a "Godly foundation," it pays little attention to the plight of dissenters like Roger Williams who exposed the contradiction between a Christian commonwealth and religious liberty.

Educated at Pembroke College, Cambridge University, Williams was a Puritan with Separatist leanings. That is, he thought the Church of England should be purified by removing the non-biblical corruptions that tainted its beliefs and practices, but he came to believe that the Church was beyond purifying. Thus, he became enamored with the ideas of Separatists who thought that they must separate themselves from the Church and establish a new church on biblical foundations. Before Puritans settled Massachusetts Bay, Separatists had established a colony at Plymouth. In 1630, Williams sailed for America, and the following year Governor John Winthrop referred to him as a "godly man." However, tensions soon arose between the two because Williams was outspoken in his criticism of the Church of England, which meant criticism of the king, and he was critical of church-state relations in Massachusetts as well as in England. He refused to become a minister at a church in Boston because, according to Winthrop, "they would not make a public declaration of their repentance for having communion with the Church of England." In addition,

Frank Lambert

Winthrop noted in his journal, Williams said that magistrates had no power whatsoever over the breach of any of the Ten Commandments in the First Table, that is, those first commandments pertaining to God and man's relation to God. Specifically, Williams spoke against Massachusetts's "blue laws," those proscribing certain activities on the Sabbath, claiming that only God could punish violators. In December 1632, Williams was brought before the General Court for his public comments regarding the authority of the King of England. Specifically, he charged Charles I with lying when he said that he was the first Christian king who had "discovered this land." Further, he charged the king with blasphemy for calling Europe "Christendom or the church world." For Winthrop, such attacks on the monarchy that had granted Massachusetts its charter were indefensible. For Williams, they were intended to deny the crown or any other government any jurisdiction over religious matters. Although Williams told the court he would desist from such attacks on the Crown's authority, he continued to speak and write against royal authority.

The court repeatedly sought to silence Williams, but he continued to speak out on what he considered to be violations of civil authorities in matters of religion. Finally, in October 1635, the court banished him from Massachusetts, having convicted him of sedition and heresy based on his spreading "diverse, new, and dangerous opinions." For Winthrop and the court, only banishment would preserve the good order of the Christian commonwealth. For Williams, Massachusetts violated his freedom of conscience and his right to speak his mind. It was a fundamental clash between the authorities who wished to uphold uniformity and the dissenter who wished to exercise his or her religious freedom.

In subsequent years Roger Williams elaborated on the ideas that resulted in his expulsion and formulated his argument for separation of church and state. In 1644, he wrote an answer to *Mr. [John] Cottons Letter Lately Printed, Examined, and Answered*, a treatise that defended Massachusetts's practice of maintaining communion with the Church of England. In his reply, Williams set forth his view that church and state ought to be completely separated and introduced the metaphor of a "wall of separation," which Thomas Jefferson would cite in 1803 and which the Christian Right sees as a deist invention, and, therefore, should be given no weight. Williams wrote:

> First the faithful labors of many Witnesses of Jesus Christ, extant to the world, abundantly proving, that the Church of the Jews under the Old Testament in the type, and the Church of the Christians under the New Testament in the Antitype, were both separate from the world; and that when they have opened a gap in the hedge or wall of Separation between the Garden of the Church and the Wilderness of the world, God hath ever broke down the wall itself, removed the Candlestick, and made his Garden a Wilderness, as at this day. And that therefore if he will ever please to restore his Garden and Paradise again, it must of necessity be walled in peculiarly unto Himself from the world, and that all that shall be saved out of the world are to be transplanted out of the Wilderness of the world, and added unto His Church or Garden.[11]

In 1651, while visiting London, Williams continued his attack on state support of religion, writing a stinging denunciation of English laws requiring subjects to support Anglican clergymen with their tithes even though some taxpayers did not subscribe to the Church's beliefs and

---

[11] Roger Williams, *Mr. Cottons Letter Lately Printed, Examined, and Answered* (London, 1644) 45.

practices. He began his attack by drawing a sharp distinction between a "civil" and a "Christian" state. The former is strictly a secular order, while the latter is a "Spiritual State of the Church of Jesus Christ." He argued that the civil state had neither the power to prevent Christians from being good Christians nor that of coercing people into becoming Christians in the first place. Moreover, Williams contended that it was "against the testimony of Christ Jesus for the civill state to impose upon the soules of the People a Religion, a Worship, [and] a Ministry."[12]

After stating what the civil state should not do regarding religious matters, Williams asked, "What is then the express duty of the civil magistrate as to Christ Jesus, His Gospel and Kingdom?" He responded that the first duty of the magistrate was to eliminate "the Civill Bars, Obstructions, Hindrances in taking off those Yoaks that pinch the very soules and consciences of men, such as yet are the payment of Tithes and the Maintenance of Ministers they have no faith in."[13]

Roger Williams's best known, and perhaps most eloquent, statement on church-state relations is his treatise, *The Bloody Tenet of Persecution for Cause of Conscience* (1644). He opened by stating that civil states have nothing to do with religion. "All civil states," he wrote, "with their officers of justice, in their respective constitutions and administrations, are...essentially civil, and therefore not judges, governors, or defenders of the Spiritual, or Christian, State and worship." Within civil states, all persons, regardless of religious leanings, should have

---

[12] See Roger Williams, *The Hirelings Ministry None of Christs, or, A Discourse Touching the Propagating the Gospel of Christ Jesus* (London, 1652).
[13] Ibid.

freedom of worship, and the state should have no powers of compulsion over one's conscience. He asserted, "It is the will and command of God that, since the coming of His Son, the Lord Jesus, a permission of the most Paganish, Jewish, Turkish or anti-Christian consciences and worship be granted to all men, in all nations and countries; and they are only to be fought against with that sword which is only, in Soul matters able to conquer, to wit; the sword of the Spirit—the Word of God." Finally, Williams explicitly denounced the principle of religious uniformity:

> God requireth not an [sic] uniformity of religion to be enacted and enforced in any civil state; which enforced uniformity, sooner or later, is the greatest occasion of civil war, ravishing consciences, persecution of Christ Jesus in His servants, and of the hypocrisy and destruction of millions of souls.... An enforced uniformity of religion throughout a nation or civil state confounds the civil and religious, denies the principles of Christianity and civility, and that Jesus Christ is come in the flesh.[14]

John Winthrop and the General Court disagreed with Williams's views on church-state relations and used the power of the state to enforce a strict uniformity. The case of Anne Hutchinson illustrates the extent to which individuals were allowed to dissent in the Christian commonwealth of Massachusetts. Anne Hutchinson was a good and faithful member of John Cotton's Puritan congregation in England. She was a Calvinist, which meant that she believed people were saved through divine election. That is, salvation was strictly the work of God's grace and not the result of the good works of the individual or the workings of the church.

---

[14] Roger Williams, *The Bloody Tenet, a Persecution, for Cause of Conscience* in Anton Stokes, ed., *Church and State in the United States*, 3 vols. (New York: Harper and Brothers, 1950), 1:196-97.

Even in England she was outspoken, a trait that was dangerous when Puritans were persecuted and doubly dangerous for a woman, who was supposed to be obedient to her husband and to the Church. In 1634, she and her husband, Will, decided to follow John Cotton to New England, and she hoped that there she would have the freedom from doctrinal error and freedom to express what she deigned to believe was the truth. Her reputation as an outspoken woman was strengthened on the trip over when she claimed clairvoyant powers, even predicting the exact time when the boat would arrive in Massachusetts. She arrived in the Christian commonwealth with great hopes for her family of fifteen children.

But, Anne Hutchinson thought for herself and that got her into trouble. She not only attended services at Cotton's meetinghouse, she took notes on sermons for later review and discussion. Her problems began when she formed a discussion group that met in her house, which became a forum for challenging what she thought were erroneous opinions being preached in Massachusetts. She accused all the ministers in the Boston area except John Cotton and John Wheelwright (her husband's brother-in-law) of preaching a "covenant of works" as opposed to a "covenant of grace." Her discussion group expanded as men and women who agreed with her met to denounce the heterodoxy. Hutchinson and her meetings attracted the attention of Governor John Winthrop, who viewed them as subversive to the good order of both church and state. Moreover, he thought that her teachings, not those of the ministers, were heretical. He accused her of the heresy of antinomianism, that is, of holding that because salvation is by grace alone under the Gospel dispensation, obligations under moral law are nullified. Further, Winthrop believed that matters of doctrine were based on a correct reading of the Bible, not on the individual's claim of divine light.

When Hutchinson refused to cease her criticism and continued her meetings despite Winthrop's orders, he summoned her to court. The trial transcript sets forth the charges:

> Mrs. Hutchinson, you are called here as one of those that have troubled the peace of the commonwealth and the churches here; you are known to be a woman that hath had a great share in the promoting and divulging of those opinions that are the cause of this trouble, and to be nearly joined not only in affinity and affection with some of those the court had taken notice of and passed censure upon, but you have spoken divers things, as we have been informed, very prejudicial to the honour of the churches and ministers thereof, and you have maintained a meeting and an assembly in your house that hath been condemned by the general assembly as a thing not tolerable nor comely in the sight of God nor fitting for your sex, and notwithstanding that was cried down you have continued the same.[15]

Winthrop's indictment of Hutchinson exposes the relation between order and liberty in the Christian commonwealth of Massachusetts. His first charge was that Hutchinson had disturbed the peace of church and state. Good order built on religious uniformity was for Winthrop the inviolate principle of the colony, and no individual had

---

[15] The transcript of Anne Hutchinson's trial is available online; see http://www.annehutchinson.com/anne_hutchinson_trial_001.htm (accessed 11 August 2012). Also, for John Winthrop's account, see *A Journal of the Transactions and Occurrences in the Settlement of Massachusetts and the Other New-England Colonies, from the Year 1630 to 1644: Written by John Winthrop, Esq; First Governor of Massachusetts: and Now First Published from a Correct Copy of the Original Manuscript* (Hartford: Elisha Babcock, 1790) 111–44.

the right to disturb that good order. For Winthrop, there was no freedom outside "ordered freedom." Second, Hutchinson was charged with dishonoring the churches by criticizing some of the ministers. For Winthrop, free speech and assembly did not extend to an individual's open censure of those called to lead congregations, especially one who dared to place her "inner light" above that of the Word of God rightly interpreted by godly ministers. And, third, Winthrop indicted Hutchinson for conduct unbecoming that of a woman. It was not befitting for a woman to conduct assemblies attended by men and women for the purpose of questioning the biblical interpretation of ministers.

In the trial before the General Court, Hutchinson's defense was that she had committed no violation at all other than exercise her God-given right of freedom of conscience. She repeatedly asked Winthrop to state the charges brought against her, refusing to recognize those that he had cited. To her, the governor's notion that she had disrupted an orderly society carried no weight for her; what was more important was the substance of her teachings. She acquitted herself very well at the trial, putting Winthrop and the court on the defensive until near the end. When the court called six ministers to testify that she had charged them with being under a covenant of works, Hutchinson replied that she had said only that they preached a covenant of works, that there was a distinction between being under such a covenant and preaching such. Hutchinson's downfall came under questioning of how she knew the things that she taught: how could she be so sure that she was right? She answered that she knew by "immediate revelation," that is, like God had spoken directly to Abraham, God's Spirit had spoken directly to her soul.[16]

Upon hearing her claim of immediate revelation, Winthrop and the court had heard enough to condemn her. Winthrop pronounced the judgment:

> The court hath already declared themselves satisfied concerning the things you hear, and concerning the troublesomeness of her spirit and the danger of her course amongst us, which is not to be suffered. Therefore if it be the mind of the court that Mrs. Hutchinson for these things that appear before us is unfit for our society, and if it be the mind of the court that she shall be banished out of our liberties and imprisoned till she be sent away, let them hold up their hands.[17]

With a minority dissent from three ministers, the judgment was affirmed and Hutchinson was banished from the Christian commonwealth of Massachusetts. For Winthrop, good order could not be maintained without religious uniformity, and direct revelation threatened uniformity. If each member of society could claim direct divine revelation, then there would be a jumble of beliefs. There can be but one source of authority and for Winthrop that was the Bible, and the Bible must be obeyed as interpreted by godly, orthodox ministers. Hutchinson and her family relocated to Roger Williams's new colony of Rhode Island, where they lived until 1643 when she and all but one of her children were killed in an Indian attack. Upon hearing of her death, Governor Winthrop supposedly said, "Proud Jezebel has at last been cast down." To him, Anne Hutchinson was a dangerous heretic; to Roger Williams she was a martyr for religious freedom.

---

[16] Ibid.
[17] Ibid.

While Roger Williams and Anne Hutchinson experienced the power of the state to curb religious dissent, Robert Keayne felt the power of the church to restrict his freedom in conducting business. Before considering the case that placed Keayne under the judgment of the church and state because of his business practices, it is necessary to understand something of his business. Keayne was a commission merchant in Boston who strove to make a profit by purchasing manufactured goods in England and making them available to consumers in New England. His world was the Atlantic market, and the rules by which he traded were those set by the market. To make a profit he had to buy goods at the lowest price he could negotiate, keep his shipping costs as low as possible, and make his merchandise available to consumers at a competitive price. In addition to supply and costs, Keayne had to consider demand for his wares. If he brought his merchandise to a market already glutted with goods, the price he could expect would be lowered. Or, if his ships arrived too late to meet demand in a given season, his merchandise would likely remain in his warehouse for a longer time.

Keayne cannot be dismissed as a merchant who cared only about profits; he also was a man of piety, and in Massachusetts Bay, profits and piety were not necessarily antithetical pursuits. Puritans believed that everyone had a particular calling from God, that is, a calling to a vocation. Not only were ministers thought to be called by God, but merchants and farmers and lawyers were called to their respective endeavors as well. Further, one was expected to pursue one's calling with faithful diligence. Indeed, the "Puritan work ethic" underscored the virtues of industry and frugality. If one worked hard and saved one's money, he or she could prosper, and prosperity was one of the outward signs that Puritans recognized as an indication of divine election. Thus, profits and piety were interrelated. However, the balance was delicate. If one became too enamored with riches or was filled with pride because of his or her accomplishments, then the pursuit of profit became a stumbling block to true piety.

Keayne first directed his attention to New England in the 1620s when he became one of the investors of the Plymouth colony that was settled by Separatists. Then in the early 1630s, he became associated with the Massachusetts Bay Company also as an investor. In 1634, the Massachusetts General Court appealed to him to use his expertise in pricing certain firearms that were about to be sent to the colony. Then, in 1635, Keayne decided to emigrate to New England. Why this prosperous merchant would leave England for the New World wilderness is unclear. John Winthrop declared that Keayne was motivated solely by religious reasons, that he had "come over for conscience's sake, and for the advancement of the Gospel here." But when one looks at Keayne's Last Will and Testament of 1653, it is hard to fathom that he could have left England without "carefully calculating his economic opportunities." As one historian put it, "Certainly Keayne was not indifferent to the fact that God would prosper the righteous and industrious in this promised land."[18]

Keayne arrived with considerable assets, having brought with him "two or 3000 lb in good estate of my owne," a sum that immediately placed him among the more prosperous freemen of Massachusetts. He quickly assumed the responsibilities expected of the "better sort"; just a few months after his arrival the Boston Town Meeting acknowledged a monetary contribution he made toward

---

[18] See Bernard Bailyn, "The Apologia of Robert Keayne," in the *William and Mary Quarterly*, 3rd series, vol. 7, no. 4 (October 1950): 571.

"building a strong battlement on Fort Hill." In March 1635, Keayne assumed his place in the Christian commonwealth by being admitted as a visible saint into the congregation of the First Church. There was, however, a cloud hanging over him that raised the suspicions of his fellow Bostonians. Some knew of his reputation for "sharp dealing and heartlessness in business [that] had preceded him to the New World." In 1639, Governor Winthrop wrote that the "corrupt practice of this man…was the more observable, because he was wealthy and sold dearer than most other tradesmen, and for that he was of ill report for the like covetous practice in England that incensed the deputies very much against him."[19]

It was in 1639 that Robert Keayne was brought before the General Court to answer charges of sharp business practices. Keayne was charged with "taking above six-pence in the shilling profit; in some above eight-pence; and, in some small things, above two for one." The matter seems trifling to modern-day sensibilities. Like other merchants, Keayne set his prices to recover his costs, all his costs, and to gain whatever the market would bear. But, the General Court found that his prices were exorbitant, perhaps what people today would call price-gouging. Such practices in the Christian commonwealth were not only deemed unlawful but sinful. Merchants were expected to conduct their businesses for the community's benefit and not solely to maximize profits. Therefore, the court fined him 200 pounds for "this sin," although they later reduced it to 80.

Winthrop knew that Keayne's business practices were probably those followed by most if not all Boston merchants, but he wanted to clarify for the whole community the moral grounds for trading. Therefore, he

---

[19] Ibid., 572.

asked John Cotton to preach a sermon on economic behavior in general and on price-setting in particular. He wanted an authoritative set of biblical principles that would govern the conduct of all merchants.

Cotton began his sermon by expressing some sympathy for Keayne. He thought there were grounds for the magistrates to show moderation in their judgment because of several extenuating circumstances. First, "there was no law in force to limit or direct men in point of profit in their trade." Second, "it is the common practice, in all countries, for men to make use of advantages for raising the prices of their commodities." Third, Keayne "was not alone in this fault"; "all men through the country, in sale of cattle, corn, labor, etc., were guilty of the like excess in prices." Fourth, although much effort had gone into finding a "certain rule" for setting fair prices, no satisfactory law had yet been found.[20]

While Cotton sympathized with Keayne's having no clear rules for conducting business, he was less sympathetic to Keayne's conduct both before and after his civil trial. After the General Court had fined him, the church of Boston investigated his behavior as a breach of Christian charity. But, instead of acknowledging his sin, Keayne once again defended his pricing practices. However, Cotton, like Winthrop, found those practices to rest on such "false principles" as, "1. That, if a man lost in one commodity, he might help himself in the price of another. 2. That if, through want of skill or other occasion, his commodity cost him more than the price of the market in England, he might then sell it for more than the price of the market in New

---

[20] See *A Journal of the Transactions and Occurrences in the Settlement of Massachusetts and the Other New-England Colonies, from the Year 1630 to 1644: Written by John Winthrop*, 189.

England, etc." Although Keayne did "with tears, acknowledge and bewail his covetous and corrupt heart," he was, in Cotton's view, insisting that his business practices were justifiable.[21]

After searching Scripture, Cotton in his sermon identified business principles that he deemed to be contradictory to biblical precepts and, therefore, false. He listed them as follows:

> 1. That a man might sell as dear as he can, and buy as cheap as he can. 2. If a man lose by casualty of sea, etc., in some of his commodities, he may raise the price of the rest. 3. That he may sell as he bought, though he paid too dear, etc., and though the commodity be fallen, etc. 4. That, as a man may take the advantage of his own skill or ability, so he may of another's ignorance or necessity. 5. Where one gives time for payment, he is to take like recompense of one as of another.

After laying out "false principles," Cotton enumerated the rules for trading:

> 1. A man may not sell above the current price, i.e., such a price as is usual in the time and place, and as another (who knows the worth of the commodity) would give for it, if he had occasion to use it: as that is called current money, which every man will take, etc. 2. When a man loseth in his commodity for want of skill, etc., he must look at it as his own fault or cross, and therefore must not lay it upon another. 3. Where a man loseth by casualty of sea, or, etc., it is a loss cast upon himself by providence, and he may not ease himself of it by casting it upon another; for so a man should seem to provide against all providences, etc., that he should never lose; but where there is a scarcity of the commodity, there men may raise their price; for now it is a

---

[21] Ibid.

hand of God upon the commodity, and not the person. 4. A man may not ask any more for his commodity than his selling price, as Ephron to Abraham, the land is worth thus much.[22]

In Keayne's case, Cotton's biblical principles of trade were applied retroactively to indict him.

For the rest of his life Keayne felt the pain of that "deepe and sharpe censure that was layd upon" him in 1639. He disagreed with the court's and the church's judgment of him as a "sharp-dealing sinner"; instead, he thought he was an honest tradesman who had been savagely libeled by his personal enemies. His case illustrates the desires of a merchant to trade according to the laws of the marketplace and the insistence of the church and state that business transactions should follow moral, not market, guidelines. The case further underscores the emptiness of the Christian Right's call for a Christian America. As Conservative Republicans they champion "free enterprise" and the "free market system." Yet, in the only concrete example of a Christian commonwealth in American history, the church insisted on the regulation of trade, including the imposition of prices. Keayne's case carries a cautionary message for those who advocate close ties between church and state: be careful for what you wish.

At about the same time Robert Keayne protested the church's interference in the exchange of goods in the marketplace, William Fiennes, First Viscount Saye and Sele (1582–1662), objected to the role of the church in political affairs. Fiennes was an English nobleman sympathetic to the Puritan cause in England. By the mid-1630s, he and other like-minded nobles despaired of the future of England and considered emigrating to America. However, Lord

---

[22] Ibid., 189–90.

Saye and Sele had heard some disturbing reports about Massachusetts Bay Colony, in particular, accusations that Governor John Winthrop and the Puritan ministers who supported him were erecting a religious tyranny. To better understand the nature of the colony, he sent a letter of Ten Demands, which once again Winthrop asked John Cotton to answer. Particularly disturbing to the nobles was word that one's civil rights in the Christian commonwealth were dependent on his being a member of a congregation, an arrangement that the nobles deemed to be a new form of tyranny. In addition to imposing a religious test for voters, there was a religious test for officeholders. While voting and office-holding in England and in the other English colonies rested on property-holding, in Massachusetts they tested on one's religious affiliation. Thus, Lord Saye and Sele sought explanations from Massachusetts leaders over the concept of freedom, and John Cotton responded with what amounted to a vigorous defense of the Massachusetts way.

At the heart of the conflict between Lord Saye and Sele and the Massachusetts Puritans was the notion of liberty, an idea important to Puritans in New England, but an idea with multiple, and sometimes conflicting, meanings. Historian Karen Kupperman argues that "the founding of puritan-sponsored colonies...revealed that the single word [liberty] covered many meanings, some of which proved to be mutually exclusive." Adventurers or investors in joint-stock companies thought that their freedom to exploit the resources of North America would result in greater freedom for all: investor, colonist, and servant, as each would be at liberty to work for his own profit. It was the lure of greater opportunity that attracted settlers in the first place, especially the chance to own their own property and thus become freemen. Property rights and economic freedom, though, depended upon good government, government that would maintain order in a hierarchical society. In addition to viewing liberty as the freedom to own land and the freedom of self-government, the Puritans in Massachusetts added another meaning of liberty: "the liberty to create a truly godly society." The result was a difference in the way Massachusetts Puritans and English Puritans viewed liberty. For the latter, liberty resulted from representatives in Parliament checking the Crown's reach for too much power. But, for the former, liberty depended not on representative government but on the "quest for godliness." Lord Saye and Sele was as committed to the "cause of true religion as the Boston leadership, but [he was] utterly unprepared to accept such a potentially devastating opening to tyranny" as could result from civil liberties depending on church membership. Massachusetts's Puritan leaders gave to the congregation the liberty to define who qualified as a "godly ruler," a policy defended by Governor Winthrop, who claimed that his people possessed "clearer light and more Libertye" to found an ideal Christian commonwealth than could any parliament or other political entity. Lord Saye and Sele "was repelled by this policy which, by placing decision-making power of the congregation above that of the state, overturned the basis of good order and true liberty."[23] Cotton's replies convinced Lord Saye and Sele that Massachusetts Bay was inhospitable for him, and he decided against residing there.

In his defense of voting practices and church-state relations in Massachusetts, John Cotton justified the

---

[23] For Lord Saye and Sele's views of liberty and Massachusetts Bay Colony, see Karen Kupperman, "Definitions of Liberty on the Eve of Civil War: Lord Saye and Sele, Lord Brooke, and the American Puritan Colonies," *The Historical Journal* 32/1 (1989): 17–33.

political preeminence of the "visible saints," that is, the church members. He began by asserting that "the word, and scriptures of God do contain a short upoluposis, or platforme, not onely of theology, but also of other sacred sciences, (as he calleth them) attendants, and handmaids thereunto, which he maketh ethicks, eoconomicks, politicks, church-government, prophecy, academy." For Cotton, the Bible was the handbook for ordering all aspects of human activity. In that sense, he was in agreement with the Christian Right who claim that the Bible is a science book and a history book, as well as a guide for spiritual life. Cotton went further: the Bible laid out how a commonwealth should be governed. "It is very suitable to God's all-sufficient wisdome, and to the fulnes and perfection of Holy Scriptures," he declared, "not only to prescribe perfect rules for the right ordering of a private man's soule to everlasting blessednes with himselfe, but also for the right ordering of a man's family, yea, of the commonwealth too, so far as both of them are subordinate to spiritual ends." He then argued that the biblical prescription for church-state relations avoids "both the churches' usurpation upon civill jurisdictions,...and the commonwealth's invasion upon ecclesiasticall administrations." His elaboration of that relationship, however, is convoluted: "God's institutions (such as the government of church and of commonwealth be) may be close and compact, and co-ordinate one to another, and yet not confounded. God hath so framed the state of church government and ordinances, that they may be compatible to any common-wealth, though never so much disordered in his frame."[24] Strictly interpreted, Cotton held that church

---

[24] Lord Saye and Sele's Ten Demands and Cotton's reply to them are found in Thomas Hutchinson, *The History of the Colony and Province of*

and state are separate but closely allied. It was that close alliance that disturbed William Fiennes.

Cotton then made his views known surrounding how government should be organized. "It is better," he opined, "that the commonwealth be fashioned to the setting forth of God's house, which is his church: than to accommodate the church frame to the civill state." Therefore, he added,

> Democracy, I do not conceive that ever God did ordain as a fit government either for church or commonwealth. If the people be governors, who shall be governed? As for monarchy, and aristocracy, they are both of them clearly approved, and directed in scripture, yet so as referreth the sovereignty to himselfe, and setteth up Theocracy in both, as the best form of government in the commonwealth, as well as in the church.[25]

Clearly, Johns Eidsmoe's argument notwithstanding, the delegates to the Federal Convention of 1787 disagreed with Cotton. Neither Scripture nor the Church served as their guide for establishing the United States as a democratic republic.

Cotton concluded his defense of Massachusetts's church-state relations by insisting that it was better to live under magistrates chosen by church members than by non-church members. He explained first that the church itself does not choose civil officers nor determine what laws they enact. The church merely prepares godly voters, who in turn choose godly rulers, who then enact the civil laws that govern the Christian commonwealth. Cotton could have

---

Massachusetts Bay, ed. L.S. Mayo, 3 vols. (1936; repr., Cambridge, MA: Harvard University Press, 1970) vol 1, appendix 3: 410–13; Cotton expresses similar views in *Discourse about Civil Government in a New Plantation Whose Design Is Religion* (Cambridge MA: Samuel Green and Marmaduke Johnson, 1663).

[25] *Discourse about Civil Government.*

added that ministers like himself frequently advised the governor concerning civil matters, especially in finding biblical justification for such civil actions as those taken against Robert Keayne. In this case, Cotton justified the restriction of the franchise to church members by citing I Corinthians 6:1-5: "which place alone seemeth to me fully to decide this question: for it plainly holdeth forth this argument: It is a shame to the church to want able judges of civill matters (as v. 5.) and an audacious act in any church member voluntarily to go for judgment, otherwhere than before the saints (as v. 1.)." That being the case, he averred, it is then "no arrogance nor folly in church members, nor prejudice to the commonwealth, if voluntarily they never choose any civill judges, but from amongst the saints, such as church members are called to be."[26] Lord Saye and Sele's response is unknown, unless one takes his remaining in England as his answer.

The challenges to the Christian commonwealth as voiced by Roger Williams, Anne Hutchinson, Robert Keayne, and Lord Saye and Sele suggest that one's happiness depended upon submission and conformity. If one complied with the strictures of church and state, life could be productive and enjoyable. Indeed, the people as a whole were industrious and prosperous, and they, at least church members, lived under laws of their own making. However, if one refused to stay in his or her prescribed place or deigned to speak out on matters of conscience or exercise freedoms set forth in the English Constitution, then those dissenters faced a united front of magistrates and ministers armed with the utter assurance of righteousness by virtue of their correct interpretation of Scripture.

---

[26] Ibid.

If one holds up Massachusetts Bay Colony as a model of a Christian state, it becomes clear that there is much reason to be suspicious of anyone's claims that America was, is, or ought to be a Christian state. Questions linger: Who defines what is Christian? According to what authority? Who monitors behavior and judges what does and does not conform to the definition of "Christian"? And what happens to those who in good conscience disagree? Christian Right "historians" ignore such questions while asserting in ahistorical terms that the United States was created as a Christian state.

Decline and Fall of the Christian Commonwealth

The Christian commonwealth of Massachusetts was a human experiment, and, alas, one that failed from pressures within and without the colony. Dissenters caused little permanent damage to the Christian commonwealth. Roger Williams and Anne Hutchinson were banished from the colony. Robert Keayne was forced to comply with Cotton's rules of trade in the "moral economy." And Lord Saye and Sele did not emigrate to Massachusetts and continue his protest against church-state relations. For the vast majority who complied with the ecclesiastical and political laws, life was good. Conformity was embraced by true believers, and they were pleased with the decisive handling of dissent.

While dissenters did minimal damage, decline in church membership posed greater threats to the Christian commonwealth. By the 1660s a growing number of those within the Puritan congregations were nominal Christians, that is, they had been baptized but were unable to demonstrate that they had been regenerated. In other words, they were not deemed to be of the Elect, the "visible saints" who had covenanted with God to create a city upon a hill. When these nominal Christians brought their children to a congregation for baptism, they were denied because of the prevailing practice of baptizing only the children of the regenerate. Ministers grew concerned that their congregations would soon be comprised of more nominal members than visible saints, thus corrupting the purity of the church. Magistrates were equally concerned about the implications for society because the congregations were the nurseries for voting citizens and officeholders.

In 1662, a special synod convened to address the problem, and the solution was the so-called Halfway Covenant. Children of non-regenerate parents could be baptized and accepted into a congregation as non-voting members, thus creating a two-tiered membership. Halfway members who failed to offer an acceptable profession of faith confirming their baptism could instead subscribe to a covenant, which read:

> I do heartily take and avouch this one God who is made known to us in the Scripture by the name of God the Father, and God the Son even Jesus Christ, and God the Holy Ghost to be my God, according to the tenor of the Covenant of Grace; Wherein he hath promised to be a God to the Faithful and their seed after them in their Generations, and taketh them to be his People, and therefore unfeighnedly repenting of all my sins, I do give up myself wholly unto this God to believe in, love, serve and Obey Him sincerely and faithfully according to this written word, against all the temptations of the Devil, the World, and my own flesh and this unto death. I do also consent to be a Member of this particular Church, promising to continue steadfastly in fellowship with it, in the public Worship of God, to submit to the Order, Discipline and Government of Christ in it, and to the Ministerial teaching, guidance and oversight of the Elders of it, and to the brotherly watch of Fellow Members: and all

this according to God's Word, and by the grace of our Lord
Jesus Christ enabling me thereunto. Amen.[27]

Reaction to the Halfway Covenant was mixed and
divided congregations. Those who approved saw it as an
important accommodation to those who were yet unable to
demonstrate that they were of the Elect. They thought it a
necessary compromise that preserved good order in society
by including everyone in the churches. Opponents, on the
other hand, viewed the covenant as a loss of purity in the
congregations and a threat to the good order of the
commonwealth. They recalled the solemn covenant that
John Winthrop had proclaimed at the colony's founding, a
covenant whereby the people promised to be submissive to
the Word of God, and to these opponents, the Halfway
Covenant was not sanctioned by Scripture.

Some ministers viewed both the Halfway Covenant
and the problem that led to it as indicators of spiritual
decline. In sermons known as "jeremiads," they lamented
the second and third generations' loss of the fervor
demonstrated by the original settlers. One of the most
quoted jeremiads is that preached by Roxbury pastor
Samuel Danforth in 1670, titled *A Brief Recognition of New-
England's Errand into the Wilderness.* He began by reminding
his audience why they and their ancestors had come to
Massachusetts in the first place. He declared,

> You have solemnly professed before God, Angels, and
> Men, that the Cause of your leaving your Country,
> Kindred, and Fathers houses, and transporting your selves
> with your Wives, Little Ones, and Substance over the vast
> Ocean into this waste and howling Wilderness, was your

---

[27] For a detailed discussion of the Halfway Covenant, see Williston
Walker, *The Creeds and Platforms of Congregationalism* (New York, 1893) 238–
87.

Liberty to walk in the Faith of the Gospel with all good Conscience according to the Order of the Gospel, and your enjoyment of the pure Worship of God according to his Institution, without humane Mixtures and Impositions.

He said that the mission was a religious one and that it was under Christ's guidance and protection. At times, God had punished the Puritans when they went astray; at others he had blessed them for their obedience. The early Puritans had chosen to obey God and consequently live under the "promise of divine Protection and Preservation." Danforth added that the Puritans had chosen "for our Portion, To sit at Christ's feet and hear his word; and whosoever complain against us, the Lord Jesus will plead for us...and say. They have chosen that good part, which shall not be taken away from them." But, alas, like God's Chosen People in the Old Testament who disobeyed God and created molten images in the Egyptian wilderness, the "chosen people" of Massachusetts did soon "forget their Errand into the Wilderness, and corrupt themselves in their own Inventions." Danforth lamented that the New England Puritans had turned aside from their original and pure motive for settlement and had embraced diverse and dangerous beliefs. Moreover, the errand had been altered as people more and more seemed to pursue profits rather than piety. They were more interested in worldly honors and riches than in spiritual ones. He concluded by calling for repentance, asking his listeners: "Do we now repent of our choice, and prefer the Honours, Pleasures, and Profits of the world before it?"[28] Only by repenting of their selfish ways

---

[28] Samuel Danforth, *A Brief Recognition of New-England's Errand into the Wilderness* (Cambridge MA: Samuel Green and Marmaduke Johnson, 1671) 5 and 18.

and returning to the obedience of God could the Puritans prosper.

The Puritans, however, faced more than spiritual decline; they faced imperial censure. When Winthrop first reviewed the Massachusetts Bay Charter, he recognized that there was no specification for where the company should reside. Other colonial charters dictated that officers of the colonizing company must reside in London, where there could be adequate royal oversight. Winthrop concluded that the omission permitted the Puritans to take their charter with them and establish their company in New England, far from royal supervision. Consequently, he and other colonial officials exercised considerable autonomy. Moreover, the Crown and Parliament were locked in a power struggle for much of the seventeenth century, culminating in civil war, followed by the execution of Charles I and the abolition of the monarchy during the 1650s. But with the restoration of the Stuarts in 1660, the Crown began to pay closer attention to Massachusetts. Several transgressions of the English constitution and English law caught the attention of royal officials. One grievance was Puritan intolerance of Anglican worshippers. A second was violation of the Navigation Acts of the 1650s, which were designed to create a closed trading system that would channel all trade between England and the American colonies into English ports only. New England merchants routinely flaunted the trade regulations, not only trading with other countries but sometimes with England's enemies. As a consequence, the Crown demanded compliance with English laws as a condition for the Puritans to keep their charter.

Puritans in Massachusetts were divided over how to respond to tightening imperial control. A Conservative faction, which included many of the most revered ministers, resisted any change whatsoever, claiming that the charter was a sacred contract that could not be rescinded and that any compromise would be disobedience to the covenant with God. A second group, led by merchants, argued for compliance with royal demands, arguing that the colony was a part of the empire and that its economic interests would likely be better protected by the crown than by the old charter. A third group sought a middle ground, willing to compromise in order to preserve some of the original charter. Unable to agree, the colonists did nothing, and in 1684 Charles II revoked the colony's charter, thus ending the official rule of the Puritans. In 1691, James II granted a new royal charter that tied Massachusetts directly to the Crown and the English Constitution.

The new charter signaled a dramatic change in Massachusetts, including the end of the Christian commonwealth. No longer would the colony's laws be based on the Bible; now they would conform to the English Constitution and English Common Law. And, perhaps more significantly, religious uniformity and the purity of religion in Massachusetts were replaced by a myriad of faiths protected by the English Act of Religious Toleration (1689). Now Anglicans and Baptists and Quakers could and did worship publicly. While still the established religion, Congregational Churches saw their influence weakened as other sects demanded, for example, that taxes for the support of religion be allotted to all churches, not just to Congregational Churches.

It is ironic that, under the new charter, the former Puritan commonwealth of Massachusetts, once the bastion of religious conformity, became the center of political freedom under the English Constitution. In a speech made in 1775, British statesman Edmund Burke explained why New England took the lead in protesting the new imperial policies of the 1760s and 1770s. He wrote that it was "the dissidence of dissent and the Protestantism of the Protestant religion" that animated the New Englanders.[29] Dissent, not conformity, became the legacy of the failed Christian commonwealth. And in another irony, it is that commitment to dissent and freedom that the Christian Right embrace in their commitment to individual freedom and free markets. Had the Christian commonwealth and its principle of uniformity become the model for the new republic in 1787, that dissent and those freedoms would have been jeopardized, just as they were in Massachusetts Bay Colony.

No doubt William Williams and Isaac Backus emphasized different aspects of the Puritan Christian commonwealths as they remembered them in 1787. Williams dwelt on the lofty purposes of the "city upon a hill" and its biblical foundations. Backus focused on what he regarded as an oppressive religious uniformity that violated liberty of conscience. Thus how they remembered the past shaped their views of the present. Christian Right "historians" not only have a selective memory of the past, they construct a past based on their preconceptions and convictions. It is a history that prefers to talk about a Christian state in the abstract without examining historical examples that offer a more disturbing story for their purposes.

---

[29] Edmund Burke, *Second Speech on Conciliation with America. The Thirteen Resolutions, The Work of the Right Honourable Edmund Burke*, 6 vols (London: Henry G. Bohn, 1854-56), I: 464-71.

3

Eighteenth-Century America:
Sacred *and* Secular

The Great Awakening struck Boston like lightning in 1740. George Whitefield, the itinerant evangelical preacher whose oratory in England had electrified audiences numbering in the tens of thousands, turned Calvinist orthodoxy on its head. Whitefield saw himself as preaching in the "good old way" of the Puritans, but his emphasis on a spiritual New Birth as "the one thing needful" weakened the Calvinist doctrine of election. For Whitefield, the only way to salvation was for the "indwelling Christ" to bring about a conversion experience within the individual; at that point he followed Calvinist thinking. However, he believed that salvation was instantaneous and that the individual could know for certain that he or she was saved. Moreover, Whitefield taught that it was experience, rather than the Bible or the Church, that was the ultimate authority in matters of redemption. In effect, his message vindicated Anne Hutchinson by agreeing with the heretic that the individual could have direct communication with God and a saving inner experience that only the individual and God could confirm.

A decade later the meaning of lightning itself in Boston was challenged. While a student at Harvard, John Adams witnessed a dramatic clash between science and religion when Bostonians reacted to Benjamin Franklin's new invention: the lightning rod. Boston Puritans had long regarded lightning as a supernatural power that the Almighty used to punish His wayward children. For Puritans, devastating fires caused by lightning were signals of God's wrath and occasioned the call for fast days, days set aside for prayer and introspection. For some time, Franklin thought that his Puritan ancestors were wrong and that lightning was a natural phenomenon. He thought it was electricity, and had all of the characteristics of electricity, which meant that it was conductive and controllable. After demonstrating his theory through the famous kite experiment, he devised rods that could be affixed to the tops of buildings to conduct electricity of lightning harmlessly to the ground. Adams applauded the invention and believed that it was a fine example of how science could benefit humankind. However, not all in Boston shared that view. Adams wrote that many objected to the lightning rod as interfering with God's own use of nature. He wrote that they "consider Thunder and Lightning as well as Earthquakes, only as Judgments, Punishments, Warnings, &c. and have no Conception of any Uses they can serve in Nature." He said that he had "heard some Persons of the highest Rank among us, say that they really thought the Erection of Iron Points, was an impious attempt to robb the almighty of his Thunder, to wrest the Bolt of Vengeance out of his Hand." For Adams, such opposition to science resulted from "the superstition, affectation of Piety, and Jealousy of new Inventions, that Inoculation to prevent the Danger of the Small Pox, and all other useful Discoveries, have met with in all ages of the World."[1]

---

[1] For Franklin's kite experiment, see Kenneth Silverman, ed.,

Whitefield and Franklin had profound impact not only on Boston but on American culture. They represented, respectively, the Great Awakening, a sacred revival of evangelical Christianity, and Enlightenment, a secular view of the world that centered on nature and human reason as the foundation of science. These two movements clashed at points, in particular points of theology, and converged at others, especially in the centrality of the individual. Both continue to influence the way that Americans view the world. American history is not an *either-or*, but a *both-and* proposition. To erase either sacred or secular influences is to distort the nation's past. That is not to say that, for any given moment, one factor is more prominent than another. Christian Right "historians" try to dismiss any secular influence on the nation's founding, but the historical record of the period confounds their efforts. Enlightenment thought had much more sway with the authors of the nation's founding documents, especially evident in Thomas Jefferson's draft of the Declaration of Independence. This chapter explores the beliefs and practices of both awakened and enlightened Americans in the eighteenth century and ends with an analysis of their relative influence on the Declaration of Independence.

Awakened and Sacred

The Great Awakening was a series of evangelical revivals that swept the Atlantic World in the mid-eighteenth century. Its message was simple and powerful: salvation is a matter of personal experience, a New Birth generated by

---

Benjamin Franklin: Autobiography and Other Writings (New York: Penguin, 1986) 212–15; for Adams's commentary, see L.H. Butterfield, ed., *Diary and Autobiography of John Adams*, 4 vols. (Cambridge MA: Belknap Press, 1961) 1:61–62.

the Holy Spirit within the individual. Such a message was revolutionary because it challenged traditional authority including that of churches, denominations, and clergymen. Moreover, revival preachers were unconventional in spreading the Gospel; they ignored parish lines and delivered extemporaneous sermons at all times and all places, including markets, racecourses, and public parks. Led by charismatic individuals like George Whitefield, Gilbert Tennent, and James Davenport, the revivals had profound influence on Americans and their culture. First, thousands of persons underwent conversion experiences. Second, their personal liberation from sin inspired them to fight for liberation from establishment laws that restricted their freedom of conscience. And, third, awakened individuals challenged the authority of religious, political, and social leaders whose morals they decried.

The Great Awakening both united and divided Americans. It united by creating a common set of experiences that transcended colonial boundaries. Persons in Georgia, for example, read about revivals in Massachusetts and saw that, although separated by a thousand miles, born-again individuals there were just like them. In a sense, the Great Awakening was the first national movement in British North America, predating the formation of the United States by forty years. But, it also divided Americans, including Christians and their churches, because not all Christians interpreted what happened as a "Work of God," as claimed by revival leaders. Some saw the revival as the work of manipulative enthusiasts who substituted their "overheated passions" for biblical truth. Perhaps most importantly, the Great Awakening undermined the idea of religious uniformity and the likelihood of a Christian state. Awakened individuals insisted on deciding religious matters for themselves and refused to submit to any government strictures or mandates.

It is ironic, then, that in his 2010 series on the "Founding Fathers," Conservative commentator and television host Glen Beck listed eighteenth-century evangelical revival preacher, George Whitefield, as "one of the Founding Fathers." Like the Christian Right "historians," Beck accused liberals with attacking the nation's founders as part of an effort to "undermine faith and religion." He included Whitefield in his series because, he argued, Whitefield was indeed one of the nation's founders and he could teach Americans "a little bit about faith and religion."[2] Beck's inclusion of Whitefield as a "Founding Father" was intended to advance the Christian Right agenda in two ways. First, it portrayed a religious figure (who, incidentally, was not an American, but a visiting evangelist from England who died six years before American independence) as instrumental in the founding of America, thus shoring up the argument that the country was founded as a Christian nation. Second, it underscored religious rather than secular ideas as defining the new nation. But when considered within historical context, the Great Awakening is the story of the individualization of American Christianity, a story that precludes the formation of any Christian state, no matter how broadly defined.

A religious awakening presupposes a religious sleep. That was the metaphor often used by evangelicals in the first third of the eighteenth century. Similar to the Puritan ministers' notion of declension, a spiritual sleep meant that the current generation had lost the fervor that had animated

---

[2] "Glenn Beck: Founders' Friday: George Whitefield." See www.foxnews.com/story/2010/05/17/glenn-beck-fonders-friday-george-whitefield/. Accessed August 20, 2013.

their ancestors. Indeed, evangelicals like Jonathan Edwards (1703–1758) of Northampton, Massachusetts, lamented how religion had grown cold and formal, that instead of embracing God's Spirit and living lives of practical piety, people were content to follow the outward manifestations of religion: church attendance, prayer, Bible-reading, etc. But Edwards also believed that periodically God sent extraordinary outpourings of His grace to sleeping saints, and on those occasions faith was renewed. Pentecost was the first of these showers of grace and the Protestant Reformation was the other. Edwards believed God had promised another and final outpouring.

By 1742, as the New England Great Awakening grew in intensity, Edwards was sure that God had begun a great work; indeed, he thought the revival was the long-expected "great Effusion of the Spirit in the latter Days" foretold in Isaiah, and that God had chosen America as the place to manifest this final outpouring of grace. Edwards began by declaring that God made "two Worlds," the "old and the new...far separated" from each other. It was the Old World that God chose for the birth of His Son and the beginning of His Church. But the Old World was also where men killed Christ and shed the blood of countless Christian martyrs. Now, Edwards argued, God has chosen the New World to bring about the "most glorious Renovation of the World." He saw a parallel between the courses of material and spiritual history. For centuries wealth in the form of gold and silver had flowed from the Old World; more recently, he noted, the New World had become the major supplier of precious metals. And so "the Course of Things in spiritual Respects will in like Manner be turn'd." He also tied America's discovery to the great work of God in spreading His grace throughout the world. He wrote, "'Tis worthy to be noted that America was discovered about the time of the

Reformation, or but little before." And now, he added, "the church's latter-day glory," as he called the Great Awakening, "is to take its rise in that new world." Finally, Edwards compared the progress of the Reformation to the solar cycle: "like the sun that rises in the east and sets in the west, so is the cause of God's providence." The Reformation arose in Europe, but it was incomplete. God promised that there would be another outpouring of His grace, and according to Edwards, writing in the 1740s, there were "abundant reasons to hope that what is now seen in America, and especially in New England, may prove the dawn of that glorious day."[3]

By identifying the revival of religion with America, Edwards contributed to the notion that America enjoyed an exceptional place in salvation history. The American Great Awakening would take its place alongside the "city upon a hill" as enduring images of God's favor on the nation, images that the Christian Right hold up as proof that America was conceived of as a Christian nation. However, those images were never accepted by all Americans and were hotly contested. We have seen how dissenters within Massachusetts Bay Colony and critics without challenged the "city upon a hill," and we now turn to how the Great Awakening produced divisions within the revival and attracted condemnation from outside.

Because the Great Awakening centered on individual experience, it is not surprising that it was never monolithic. Rather, it had many and diverse followers who crafted competing expressions of revival. Most revivalists, however, fell into one of two categories: moderates and

---

[3] C.C. Goen, ed., *Jonathan Edwards: The Great Awakening*, vol. 4 of *The Works of Jonathan Edwards*, ed. John E. Smith et al. (New Haven: Yale University Press, 1972) 355–58.

radicals, with the distinction resting on how awakeners viewed the working of God's Spirit. To moderates, like Whitefield, the awakening was first a work of God that conformed to recognizable biblical signs. The Bible set forth how God's Spirit would operate during seasons of extraordinary outpourings of grace, and moderates were suspicious of those who claimed direct divine revelation or inward impulses that took precedence over biblical authority. Moreover, moderates believed that God was a God of order and that the revivals should be led by God-called, educated clergy. They found disturbing some of the demonstrative behavior of persons overwrought by their conversion experience, such as convulsions, fits, shouts, laughing, dancing, and fainting.

Radicals came to the conclusion that only the converted embraced "pure and undefiled" religion and they should separate themselves from all other Christians. Thus they left their old congregations and formed separate churches, which, they declared, were the only true Christian bodies. One radical, James Davenport, invited his followers to burn all books, including some Christian classics and some works by moderate revivalists, that opposed the "true" faith as he and they defined it. When the books went up in flames, Davenport shouted, "Thus the Souls of the Authors of those Books, those of them that are dead, are roasting in the Flames of Hell."[4] Radical Separatists had no doubt whatsoever about their beliefs. They were right and they knew it. Indeed, one congregation in Mansfield, Massachusetts, vowed in its Confession of

---

[4] *Boston Weekly Post-Boy*, 28 March 1743.

Faith that "all doubting in a believer is sinful, being contrary to the command of God."[5]

Even within moderate ranks, there was sometimes profound disagreement between pastor and congregation over the question of salvation. In 1751, Jonathan Edwards was dismissed from his congregation at Northampton, and the reason underscores the argument that the Great Awakening was never monolithic. The dispute had to do with qualifications for church membership. As the revival waned, a majority of his church members wanted to return to the practice stipulated by the Halfway Covenant, which set baptism as the sole criterion. Edwards wanted the candidate's beliefs, experiences, and behavior to be more thoroughly investigated before granting admission to the congregation. The split ended with his being fired by a vote of about 10 to 1. What was played out in Northampton was repeated wherever the Awakening had occurred. Some wanted a higher standard of church membership, while others wanted to return to the old way.

In addition to differences within the ranks of the awakened, the Great Awakening divided denominations. The Congregational Churches divided into two groups: the pro-revival New Lights and the anti-revival Old Lights. The latter charged the former with introducing dangerous new tenets, in particular, that of "enthusiasm." Enthusiasm was the belief that an individual had direct inspiration from God, just as Anne Hutchinson had claimed more than 100 years earlier. Further, Old Lights accused New Lights with bringing disorder into the churches, an accusation stemming from the behavior of some New Lights, who in

---

[5] Cited in Joseph Tracy, *The Great Awakening: A History of the Revival of Religion in the Time of Edwards and Whitefield* (Boston: Charles Tappen, 1841) 317–18.

the throes of conversion would sometimes fall to the ground or dance or laugh or sing aloud. Old Lights charged New Lights with Separatism, that is, with encouraging converts to separate from their old congregations and organize new ones according to New Light beliefs. For their part, New Lights viewed Old Lights as being unconverted. Sometimes the charges denied that Old Lights were even Christians. In a rash statement made as he departed New England in 1741, Whitefield implied that the Harvard faculty knew no more of Christianity than did "Mahomet."[6]

Because of the individualistic nature of the Great Awakening and the many interpretations of what it meant, America moved closer toward a broad and diverse marketplace of religion where no single expression of Christianity prevailed. Moreover, the revival created a religious culture where religious liberty, not religious uniformity, was paramount. Thus, a generation before the founders drafted a constitution for the United States, the Great Awakening had rendered it virtually impossible to create a Christian state. Instead, individuals, not the state, would decide the place and character of religion in the new republic.

If the contested nature of the Great Awakening meant that evangelicals could not or would not agree on a single conception of a Christian state, the Enlightenment and its religion, deism, ensured that the United States would not be defined as a Christian state. While the Christian Right accuse modern-day secularists of challenging America's Christian heritage, 250 years ago Jonathan Edwards blamed deists of his day. He warned his fellow evangelicals that the greater danger came not from disagreements within their

---

[6] For Whitefield's attacks on Harvard, see *Whitefield's Journals* (London: Banner of Truth Trust, 1998) 324, 462.

ranks, but from deists who denied the divinity of Jesus and who questioned the authority of the Bible. Deism was the religion embraced by some devotees of Enlightenment, and while nearly all deists placed reason above revelation, they were no more monolithic than were the awakened. Nonetheless, Edwards tarred them all with the same brush. He described deists as those who

> [w]holly cast off the Christian religion, and are professed infidels. They are not like the Heretics, Arians, Socinians, and others, who own the Scriptures to be the word of God, and hold the Christian religion to be the true religion, but only deny these and these fundamental doctrines of the Christian religion: they deny the whole Christian religion. Indeed they own the being of a God; but they deny that Christ was the son of God, and say he was a mere cheat; and so they say all the prophets and apostles were; and they deny the whole Scripture. They deny that any of it is the word of God. They deny revealed religion, or any word of God at all; and say that God has given mankind no other light to walk by but their own reason.[7]

Enlightened and Secular

For the Christian Right, Enlightenment is a bad word, and they try mightily to dismiss its influence on the founding of the republic. But for many in eighteenth-century America, including the most iconic of the nation's founders, Enlightenment was the intellectual pathway to declaring independence and establishing a constitution based on popular sovereignty.

Enlightenment offered people of the eighteenth century a new way of thinking about the world, humans, and even God. It challenged traditional authority and

---

[7] See Jonathan Edwards, *A History of the Work of Redemption* ([Boston: Draper and Folso, 1783) 81–82.

encouraged individuals to use their reason to understand the world and how it worked. It was optimistic in its belief in progress based on human understanding. The assumption was that nature operated according to laws, and that humans could fathom those laws and use them to bend nature to human needs. Franklin's control of lightning illustrates the idea. Enlightenment was expressed in a number of countries and took on local characteristics, such as the French Enlightenment, the German Enlightenment, the Scottish Enlightenment, but all shared a particular outlook. In 1784, Immanuel Kant offered a definition that cut across national boundaries:

> Enlightenment is man's emergence from his self-imposed immaturity. Immaturity is the inability to use one's understanding without guidance from another. This immaturity is self-imposed when its cause lies not in lack of understanding, but in lack of resolve and courage to use it without guidance from another. Sapere Aude! [dare to know] "Have courage to use your own understanding!"— that is the motto of enlightenment.[8]

Enlightenment had a profound influence on America's founders. It liberated them from traditions that sought to define and limit the place of the individual in society. Further, it challenged existing ways of thinking about nature, history, religion, monarchy, and freedom. Enlightenment influence on the founders can be illustrated by examining how John Adams and Thomas Jefferson imbibed its ideas.

---

[8] Kant's essay first appeared in German as *"Beantwortung der Frage: Was ist Aufklärung?"* in the *Berlinische Monatsschrift* (*Berlin Monthly*), ed. Friedrich Gedike and Johann Erich Biester (December 1784): 115. For an online transcript in English, see http://theliterarylink.com/kant.html (accessed 11 August 2012).

It was the notion of free-thinking that best describes how Enlightenment shaped many of America's founders, including Thomas Jefferson, John Adams, and James Madison. Like John Locke, they believed that the principles of Enlightenment applied to human society as well as to nature, and that a careful, reasoned approach to government could curb the worst appetites of human nature and enable Americans to establish a republic based on the popular sovereignty. In their view, everything was subject to questioning, including such revered sources of authority as churches, clergymen, and even the Bible. They were not anti-religion; indeed they all thought Jesus' moral teachings to be sublime. But they also believed that those teachings had been corrupted by human-constructed religious institutions and creeds. Again, Kant captures their viewpoint in his discussion of the pastor-scholar. Kant prefaced his comments by declaring, "Nothing is required for this enlightenment, however, except freedom; and the freedom in question is the least harmful of all, namely, the freedom to use reason publicly in all matters." The pastor-scholar discovers that when preaching as a pastor, he is constrained by the beliefs of the church he represents and is not, therefore, free to pursue truth as his conscience directs. But, in his study he is free to question everything, including that which his church prohibits. American founders questioned received wisdom and authority, in public as well as in private.

For John Adams the math simply did not work. That is, the Trinitarian claim that one is three and three is one made no sense whatsoever to him, and he rejected it. In doing so, he did not reject divine revelation, nor did he reject Christianity; indeed, he affirmed both. But Adams insisted in a letter to Thomas Jefferson that "the human understanding is a revelation from its Maker" and that nature is a revelation of "Nature's God." And, according to the revelations of human understanding and nature, two plus two equals four. He also believed that the Bible contained revelatory truth about God and provided a guide for moral behavior, but he thought that the Bible had been corrupted by translators, monks, and theologians. Thus, the teachings of Scripture had to be sifted through the sieve of human reason and the laws of nature, and that which did not correspond had to be cast out or explained. Truth, he insisted, was known only to God, but humans could approach divine truth through rational investigation of God's handiwork, not through frightful prophecies and wondrous miracles contained in Scripture and promulgated by Christian theologians, acting singly or in counsels. He especially railed against Calvinists who depicted God as one who created "innumerable millions, to make them miserable forever for his own glory." And, Adams lamented that belief in the Trinity was a condition of civil liberties; dissenters who denied the Trinity in England and in some of the colonies were excluded from political offices and from universities.[9]

In his reply, Jefferson expressed broad agreement with Adams. In particular, he agreed with Adams's assertion that "the human understanding is a revelation from its Maker." He then told Adams how he had applied his human understanding to the Bible, which, like Adams, he

---

[9] Material in this section is adapted from a paper I submitted for a conference on "John Adams & Thomas Jefferson: Libraries, Leadership, and Legacy" in Charlottesville, Virginia, held 21–27 June 2009. The paper is titled, "'A FREE INQUIRY' under the Authority of the People: John Adams and Thomas Jefferson on Religion." For Adams's comments on the trinity, see Bruce Braden, *"Ye Will Say I Am No Christian": The Thomas Jefferson/John Adams Correspondence on Religion, Morals, and Values* (New York: Prometheus Books, 2006) 90–91.

thought to be filled with corruptions. Jefferson said that to get to the sublime morals taught by Jesus, one must first pare off what "Platonising" theologians have ascribed to Jesus and get to the "very words only of Jesus." He informed Adams, "I have performed this operation for my own use, by cutting verse by verse out of the printed book, and arranging, the matter which is evidently his, and which is as easily distinguishable as diamonds in a dunghill."[10] This radical excision, for Jefferson, resulted in the essence of Christianity: the moral teachings of Jesus.

Adams's renunciation of the Trinity and Jefferson's redaction of the Bible illustrate much about their religious views. Both were freethinkers, that is, they fashioned for themselves their own religious beliefs, rejecting the teachings of church tradition and viewing with skepticism the thoughts of theologians. In shaping their views they relied upon their own reason and on an expanded view of revelation. To each, science was central in understanding God's creation, and by extension, God as Creator. So not only were science and faith compatible, science was the vehicle for forming one's faith. Both Adams and Jefferson subscribed to the belief that religion was a matter between God and each individual and that God had created humans with free minds and expected them to use their reason to come to right belief. While they agreed on much, they disagreed on such points as miracles and the divine ordering of society. They rejected any government role in religion other than that of protecting the free exercise of religion. While these Trinity-denying, Bible-editing men were freethinkers, their thoughts led them to embrace

---

[10] Lester Cappon, ed., *The Adams-Jefferson Letters: The Complete Correspondence Between Thomas Jefferson and Abigail and John Adams*, 2 vols. (Chapel Hill: University of North Carolina Press, 1959) 2:384.

Christianity, not the Christianity of any Church or of any theological school, to be sure, but Christianity of their own making.

John Adams's disposition and education led him away from the Calvinism of his upbringing. The Congregational Church that baptized John Adams was rooted in Calvinism, a branch of Protestantism that centered on an all-powerful God who alone was responsible for an individual's salvation. No doubt he learned the rudiments of Calvinism from the acrostic "TULIP" that Puritan parents and teachers used to teach the faith. It was a distillation of the articles of faith adopted at the Synod of Dort in 1610:

T – Total depravity of humans; Sin results in depravity and renders people incapable of working out their own salvation.

U – Unconditional predestination; Though all deserve damnation for their sins, God elects some for salvation, selecting them out of his good grace and not because of their good works.

L – Limited atonement; Christ's sacrificial death was for the atonement of the elect only.

I – Irresistible grace; Election, or the gift of grace, cannot be chosen or rejected.

P – Perseverance of saints; The Elect are secure and cannot fall from grace.

John Adams was drilled in the catechism at home, church, and school. When he went to a "Dame School," an academy for boys and girls, he studied *The New England Primer*, a combination reader, hornbook, and catechism reinforcing such tenets of faith as "In

Adam's fall, we sinned all." Deacon Adams hoped that his son would become a minister, and so he sent John to Harvard to prepare for the parish ministry. But, when John entered Harvard in 1751 at the age of 15, he encountered a new world. Harvard had traditionally followed the "aristocratic tradition of European higher education" and offered its students the classical subjects of Latin, Greek, rhetoric, and logic that they had begun in Latin schools. But in the generation before John's arrival, Harvard had embraced the new thinking of the Enlightenment and had added the natural sciences, natural philosophy, and moral philosophy to the curriculum. In addition, the method of teaching had undergone a significant change. No longer did a tutor shepherd a student through an entire class throughout his college years. Now professorships were specialized, which meant that students encountered scholars with a particular expertise. Thus, when Adams arrived, Harvard offered a more liberal education that confronted students with different, and sometimes competing, ways of viewing the world. While Harvard had once been a seminary turning out ministers for the Congregational Churches, that was no longer the case when Adams attended. Influenced by the "secular winds of the eighteenth-century Enlightenment" that was blowing across Massachusetts, and especially across the Harvard campus, more students were opting for careers in law or medicine than in the church.

One incident during Adams's second year of college illustrates how the new learning, especially that of science, shaped his religious views. It was then that he saw firsthand a clash between science and theology in explaining the world. Professor Edward Wigglesworth, Professor of Divinity, defended revealed faith from the encroachments of Newtonian math and science. He told his students they should remember that "God in his infinite wisdom had opened more than one road to knowledge." He specifically mentioned logic as one avenue, and observation and experimentation as the other. Logic, particularly Ramist logic, had long been the method by which Christian ministers extracted truth from the revealed Word of God. Moreover,

Wigglesworth added, God called certain people to undertake the task of unlocking those great truths for His people. John Winthrop, Professor of Natural Philosophy, offered Adams another way of thinking about truth. He told Adams and his classmates that in his "apparatus chamber," or science laboratory, theology or dogma or a priori propositions held no weight. Nothing, including biblical teachings about the world, counted except that which could be proven by observation and experimentation.[11] To Adams the scientific way of understanding the natural world and its Creator made more sense than did the traditional way of relying on biblical interpretation, and it held greater potential for making the world a better place to live.

As Adams approached graduation he still had not decided on a career. He had, however, ruled out the ministry. Though his father wanted him to become a pastor, and Adams wanted to please his father, John did not hold the profession in high esteem. As he followed the seemingly endless ecclesiastical and theological squabbles in Massachusetts, he came to regard preachers as dogmatic and bigoted. He equated the ministry with "banality and inefficacy" and spoke of pastors as "effeminate" and "unmanly." Moreover, John had enough self-awareness to

---

[11] Catherine Drinker Bowen, *John Adams and the American Revolution* (New York: Little, Brown and Componay, 1949) 82–84.

believe that he was ill-suited for the parish, that he was too impatient, opinionated, and egotistical to be a caring pastor who called on his parishioners when they were sick or admonished them to pay their tithes. So, after a miserable year in a Worcester classroom as a teacher, John Adams decided to pursue a career in law.

While John Adams came of age within the strict Calvinist orthodoxy of the Congregational Churches of New England, Thomas Jefferson was reared within a far more liberal Church of England that blended the sacred and the secular. By the time the young Jefferson attended services in Albemarle County, Virginia, the Anglican Church was "long past the great age of Calvinist influence," and had adopted an "unabashedly moderate stance on the question of human nature." Far from the dark portrayal of humans that Adams heard from preachers, Jefferson grew up seeing people in a much more positive light. One Anglican missionary, Thomas Barton, lampooned Calvinists' negativism: "Instead of instructing the people to 'serve the Lord with gladness' and to have 'joy in the Holy Ghost,' these miserable teachers advance a gloomy and dreadful religion which has...made many [listeners] fitter objects for a Hospital than a Church." According to one historian, the Church of England that nurtured Thomas Jefferson combined "rationalism, moralism, and piety." Parishioners were taught that the world was an understandable place, not one filled with sudden surprises, such as bolts of lightning hurled at sinners by an angry God. Indeed, by studying nature, one could gain an understanding of the Creator. The chief goal of Anglicans was to live a good life, one that conformed to Christian moral teachings.[12]

The quality of Thomas Jefferson's early education can best be described as mixed. As did most gentlemen planters in mid-eighteenth-century Virginia, Peter Jefferson placed his son with a tutor who was expected to initiate his charges in classical education with an emphasis on Greek and Latin. Unfortunately, young Thomas fell under the tutelage of William Douglas, a Scotsman who was barely competent in classic languages, and his French, tainted by a heavy Scottish accent, was little better.

Fortunately, Thomas at age 14 found a much more able teacher in the Reverend James Maury. Maury had attended William & Mary and had returned to England to take Holy Orders. He was a man of piety though he had little use for evangelical enthusiasts, especially itinerant preachers who paid no attention to parish lines and preached where they would. In particular, he objected to their appeal to listeners' emotions and to their attacks on those who espoused a different theology, namely, that of Anglican ministers. Maury was an excellent teacher, one whom Jefferson, as an adult, praised for the "correctness of his classical scholarship." Maury offered more than an education in the classics; he, in the spirit of the Enlightenment, led his students into a study of their native tongue and into an exploration of modern as well as ancient literature.[13]

Five years after John Adams graduated from Harvard, Thomas Jefferson entered the College of William and Mary at the age of 17. It was at college, as it had been for Adams, that Jefferson developed his independent mind. William

---

[12] Jon Butler, *Awash in a Sea of Faith: Christianizing the American People* (Cambridge MA: Harvard University Press, 1990) 167–68.

[13] Dumas Malone, *Jefferson and His Time: Jefferson the Virginian* (Boston: Little, Brown and Company, 1948) 40–45.

and Mary in 1760 was a tiny college boasting a faculty that numbered seven and a student body that totaled no more than 100. Students were enrolled in one of four schools: the grammar school, which was a preparatory school; the Indian school, where a handful of Native Americans attended; the divinity school, which Jefferson would later help abolish; and the philosophy school, where Jefferson was enrolled. The philosophy faculty consisted of two members, one of which was William Small, who would have the greatest influence on Jefferson. With the exception of Small, the William and Mary faculty were Anglican clergymen. In about half of Jefferson's courses, Small was his instructor, and he lectured over a wide range of subjects including science, ethics, rhetoric, and belles letters. Small introduced his best-known student to the "expansion of science" and the limitless possibilities that it represented.

Thomas Jefferson embodied the Enlightenment. While at William and Mary he embarked upon a lifelong quest for knowledge, not the knowledge that others handed down or the received lore from tradition, but that which came from rigorous, sustained study. As one biographer put it, no New England Calvinist was more self-disciplined than he was, but he pursued his quest for knowledge not simply as a duty to learn, but for the "infinite delight" he experienced in understanding the physical and social world about him. Under Small's guidance, the young Jefferson came to see that intellectual freedom was the key to true knowledge, that is, a mind rid of all encumbrances that would impede free inquiry. To embark on his journey for knowledge, the first major obstacle that he had to clear was the doctrine of "supernatural revelation." Religious leaders based their claims on supernatural revelation found in Holy Scriptures, and they insisted that that revelation was beyond challenge. It must be accepted without question. That attitude flew in the face of Jefferson's enlightened education that led him to question everything. It did not mean that he did not believe in God; in fact, he always expressed a firm belief in God, especially as Creator. But it did mean that he insisted on arriving at that belief on his own, through the use of his reason. A sentence that he copied in his "Literary Bible" captures the sentiment: "No hypothesis," he copied from Lord Bolingbroke, "ought to be maintained if a single phenomenon stands in direct opposition to it."[14] All biblical claims were included in that sweeping statement.

At about the same time that young Jefferson was questioning the very foundation of the Christian faith, Adams was questioning one of its central doctrines. Already disposed to look askance at the theological contentions of Calvinist ministers, Adams by age 21 had become a freethinker who filtered all religious doctrines through the sieve of his own reason. He came to see Jonathan Mayhew, Pastor of the West Church in Boston, as one whose views made sense to him. Mayhew rejected Calvinism and taught instead a "theology of virtue." He had no use for "metaphysical niceties" and thought that faith was of importance only to the degree that it promoted good works. One of the "metaphysical niceties" that he jettisoned was that of the "Divinity and Satisfaction of Jesus Christ." That is, he did not believe Jesus was divine nor did he believe that he died a sacrificial death to atone for the sins of humankind and thus satisfy God's need for justice. Certainly Mayhew's ideas were far from universally accepted; indeed, Adams said they were "not generally approved." Adams, however, was drawn to them. He recalled that he and a Major Greene on one occasion "fell into some conversation" about Mayhew's rejection of the

---

[14] Cited in ibid., 103–106.

doctrine of Christ's Divinity and Satisfaction. Adams was unconvinced by Greene's argument that "a mere creature, or finite Being, could not make Satisfaction to infinite Justice, for any Crimes," adding that "these things are very mysterious." Adams wrote in the margin next to that entry in his diary: "Thus mystery is made a convenient Cover for absurdity."[15]

Thus, as Adams and Jefferson completed their formal education and embarked on careers of law and public service, they had already established the foundations for their more mature reflections on religion. Each could be described as a freethinker. Each was a devotee of the new science associated with the Enlightenment. And each was skeptical, if not hostile, to theological and biblical claims that religious leaders insisted must be accepted on faith alone.

While "orthodox" Christians, whom Adams and Jefferson called sectarians, based their beliefs on the authority of Holy Scripture and Church teachings, Adams and Jefferson expanded on what was authoritative. They, too, looked to the Bible for guidance in living a moral life, but they also insisted on interpreting Scripture according to the light of reason. In one respect, they were similar to the sectarians, who also insisted on their own biblical interpretations as being the right reading. Adams declared that the "Bible was the best book in the World. It contains more of my little Phylosophy than all the Libraries I have seen." But, Adams also thought that the biblical text had been corrupted in translation. To his son John Quincy, he asked, "What do you call the 'Bible'? The translation by King James the first. More than half a Catholick.... What Bible? King James's? The Hebrew? The Septuagint? The

---

[15] Butterfield, ed., *Diary and Autobiography of John Adams*, 1:6.

Vulgate?...Which of the thirty thousand variantia are the Rule of Faith?"[16] His point was that the individual must use reason and judgment in selecting and interpreting a text.

But Adams and Jefferson looked beyond Scripture to understand God. Nature was a text written by the Creator and was thus the clearest window into the mind of God. History was another text that revealed to them God's Providence. Each believed that while individuals must make enlightened choices, the grand sweep of history remained in God's hands. Further, they believed that God had instilled in humans two means for understanding revelation and guiding conduct. One was reason. As Jefferson advised his nephew Peter Carr in 1787, "Fix reason firmly in her seat, and call to her tribunal every fact, every opinion. Question with boldness even the existence of a God; because, if there be one, he must more approve of the homage of reason, than that of blindfolded fear." In addition to reason, God had implanted a "moral sense" in every individual, an innate moral compass that was reliable in guiding conduct. Again, in his letter to Carr, Jefferson wrote, "Man was destined for society. His morality, therefore, was to be formed to this object. He was endowed with a sense of right and wrong, merely relative to this. This sense is as much a part of his nature, as the sense of hearing, seeing, feeling; it is the true foundation of morality." Jefferson saw the moral sense as the basis for claims for human equality; all have common sense, and with it they, whether a "ploughman [or] a professor," can decide the right thing to do.[17] While the moral sense could no doubt be misleading or even overridden in individual instances,

---

[16] Cited in Hutson, *Founders on Religion*, 23, 26.

[17] Thomas Jefferson, letter to his nephew Peter Carr, from Paris, 10 August 1787; Merrill D. Peterson, ed., *Thomas Jefferson: Writings* (New York: Library of America, 1994) 900–906.

acting within large numbers of people over time, it could be relied on to prompt persons to exercise sound moral judgment.

From that set of beliefs, each distilled them into a creed of his personal beliefs. Adams and Jefferson vowed that they were Christians, but they insisted on defining their beliefs. Adams expressed his faith succinctly: "The love of God and his Creation, Delight, Joy, Tryumph, Exultation in my own existence,...are my religion." Late in his life, in a letter to Jefferson he said that after reading countless books on religion and philosophy, "they have made no Change in my moral or religious Creed, which has for 50 or 60 Years been contained in four short Words 'Be just and good.'" He had little use for sectarian dogmatism. "Ask me not, then," he wrote, "whether I am a Catholic or Protestant, Calvinist or Arminian. As far as they are Christians, I wish to be a fellow disciple with them all."[18]

Jefferson agreed with Adams's succinct creed. In his reply, Jefferson declared, "The result of your 50 or 60 years of religious reading in the four words 'be just and good' is that in which all our enquiries must end." Adams did not want anyone to think that he had rejected Christianity because he rejected much of what passed as orthodox theology. He declared his devotion to "Christianity in its Purity," while denouncing "its Corruptions." Stripped of all its corruptions, Christianity was about morality: "The Ten Commandments and The Sermon on the Mount contain my Religion." Like Adams, Jefferson believed that the sum of religion was moral behavior, not confessed belief. He declared that he was a Christian "in the only sense [Christ] wished any one to be; sincerely attached to his doctrines, in preference to all others; ascribing to himself every human

---

[18] Charles Francis Adams, ed., *The Works of John Adams*, 10:67.

excellence; and believing he never claimed any other."[19] Christian Right "historians" claim that while Jefferson was a deist, toward the end of his life he became a Christian. However, Jefferson's own words contradict that claim. In 1817, a biographer asked Jefferson to explain the "change in my religion much spoken of in some circles." In a letter to Adams, Jefferson said that that statement assumed that people knew what his religion was in the first place. Jefferson's answer to the biographer illustrates how close his creed was to Adams's: "My answer was 'say nothing of my religion.' It is known to my god and myself alone. Its evidence before the world is to be sought in my life. If that has been honest and dutiful to society, the religion which has regulated it cannot be a bad one." Jefferson saw his creed as the opposite of that of most Protestants, especially Calvinists. "My fundamental principle," he wrote in 1819, "would be the reverse of Calvin's, that we are to be saved by our good works which are within our power, and not by our faith which is not within our power."[20]

The God that Adams and Jefferson embraced was what they regarded to be the one and only God, Creator of the universe. They referred to God in deist terms, that is, the language of the Enlightenment that emphasized God as Creator. Adams called God "a moving Power," "the Supream Intelligence," and "the Architect."[21] He thought that ascribing divinity to Jesus was an affront to God: "An Incarnate God!!! An eternal, selfexistent, omnipresent omniscient Author of this stupendous Universe, suffering on a Cross!!! My Soul starts with horror, at the Idea, and it has stupefied the Christian World. It has been the Source of

---

[19] Cappon, ed., *The Adams-Jefferson Letters*, 409, 494, 499, 506.

[20] Cited in Hutson, *Founders on Religion*, 100.

[21] Cappon, ed., *The Adams-Jefferson Letters*, 411.

almost all the Corruptions of Christianity." [22] Jefferson, in the familiar language of his version of the Declaration of Independence, referred to the Almighty as "nature's god" and "supreme judge of the world."[23] Absent is any discussion of Jesus as a member of the godhead, including such doctrines as the Incarnation, the Virgin Birth, Atonement, Salvation, Redemption, and Resurrection. To both men, Jesus was a man, a moral teacher whose ethical system is worthy of emulation. He was not the Son of God who was co-eternal with God and came to earth as long-awaited Messiah to save "lost" souls.

Indeed, both men expressed their beliefs in negative as well as in positive terms. That is, they stated explicitly what they did not believe. In one of their last letters, Jefferson denounced Calvinism:

> I can never join Calvin in addressing his god. He was indeed an atheist, which I can never be; or rather his religion was daemonism. If ever man worshiped a false God, he did. The Being described in his five points, is not the God whom you and I acknowledge and adore, the Creator and benevolent Governor of the world; but a daemon of malignant spirit. It would be more pardonable to believe in no God at all, than to blaspheme Him by the atrocious attributes of Calvin. Indeed, I think every Christian sect gives a great handle to atheism by their general dogma that without a revelation, there would not be sufficient proof of the being of God. Now one-sixth only are supposed to be Christians; the other five-sixths, who do not believe in the Jewish and Christian revelation, are without knowledge of the existence of a God![24]

---

[22] Cited in Hutson, *Founders on Religion*, 121.

[23] See Garry Wills, *Inventing America: Jefferson's Declaration of Independence* (New York: Doubleday and Company, 1979) 374, 379.

[24] See Braden, *"Ye Will Say I Am No Christian,"* 220–21.

Near the end of his life Jefferson expressed the conviction that he and Adams would meet again in a future life, while at the same time denouncing fundamental doctrines of Christian orthodoxy. In August 1823, Jefferson confessed his faith in God and in an afterlife where former acquaintances would be rejoined. He said that he awaited with more readiness than reluctance a reunion with "our ancient colleagues." At the same time, he railed against what he considered to be the absurdity of the Trinity and the Virgin Birth. He rejected the interpretation of Logos as "Word" and the Christian interpretation that, therefore, the Word, or Christ, had been with God from before all time. Rather, he interpreted Logos as "Reason" and insisted that that "explains rationally the eternal pre-existence of God, and His creation of the world." He also rejected the Virgin Birth. Jefferson wrote, "[T]he greatest enemies to the doctrines of Jesus are those calling themselves the expositors of them, who have perverted them for the structure of a system of fancy absolutely incomprehensible." He said that the day would come when the "mystical generation of Jesus, by the Supreme Being as His Father, in the womb of a virgin, will be classed with fable of the generation of Minerva in the brain of Jupiter."[25]

Adams and Jefferson disagreed on several points. One was the nature of God. Jefferson was a materialist and believed that God was not spirit but had material existence; indeed, he thought it was atheism to believe in God only as spirit. Adams expressed the orthodox view of God as immaterial being. The two men also differed on the idea of miracles. Adams believed that the Creator was fully capable of intervening in the created order in supernatural ways. Jefferson dismissed miracles, arguing that humans believed

---

[25] Ibid., 223–24.

in them out of ignorance of the laws of nature. Adams and
Jefferson disagreed on the nature of man. Jefferson believed
that man was basically good and, with rigorous application
of reason, perhaps perfectible. Adams scoffed at the notion
of perfectibility, again hewing closer to the orthodox
Christian view of man as sinner. They disagreed on sources
of moral inspiration. Jefferson was a more systematic
student of ancient philosophers and therefore more willing
to include their ideas in his eclectic moral perspective than
was Adams. Adams was more critical of Enlightenment
thinkers, especially the French. After reading a volume of
letters on the amelioration of society and manners in
France, he wrote Jefferson, "I should think the age of reason
has produced nothing much better than the Mahometans,
the Mamalukes, or the Hindoos, or the North American
Indians."[26]

Secular and *Sacred: The Individual and Individual Liberty*

Christian Right "historians" assert that America's founding
documents bear the indelible stamp of Christianity and not
that of secular thought, particularly Enlightenment thought,
as academic historians have found. Context is key in
understanding those documents: why and how they were
produced, when and under what circumstances, and by
whom and according to what intellectual framework. In
historical investigation, one must pay attention to particular
people acting at specific moments. It matters who the
historical actors were and when they were making their
imprint on the past. An analysis of the Declaration of
Independence within historical context features Americans
who were greatly influenced by Enlightenment thought and

---

[26] Cappon, ed., *The Adams-Jefferson Letters*, 2:533.

who used those ideas to justify the radical act of severing ties with Britain.

On 7 June 1776, Richard Henry Lee of Virginia proposed in the Second Continental Congress that the thirteen colonies should declare their independence from Britain. His resolution read as follows:

> Resolved, That these United Colonies are, and of right ought to be, free and independent States, that they are absolved from all allegiance to the British Crown, and that all political connection between them and the State of Great Britain is, and ought to be, totally dissolved. That it is expedient forthwith to take the most effectual measures for forming foreign Alliances. That a plan of confederation be prepared and transmitted to the respective Colonies for their consideration and approbation.

The reality behind the resolution was grim. First, the colonies were already at war with Britain. For more than a year, they had been engaged in some of the fiercest fighting of the War for Independence. Second, the previous December, George III had declared the colonies to be in a state of rebellion and therefore no longer under his protection. Third, Lee and his fellow Congressmen recognized that they had to have foreign help in defeating Britain; the colonies had no navy and a largely untrained army. Thus, part of his resolution was to secure an alliance, and because of her enmity with Britain, France was the most likely choice. The Declaration of Independence, then, was a belated formal statement reflecting the realities the colonies faced. Six months earlier, Thomas Paine in *Common Sense* had urged the colonists to declare independence, not just from George III, but from monarchy itself. Indeed, before Congress finally declared independence on 2 July 1776, individual colonies, towns, artillery companies, and artisan guilds had published nearly eighty resolutions and declarations of American rights.

Congress appointed a committee to draft the Declaration of Independence, and three of the five appointed were imbued with Enlightenment thought: John Adams, Thomas Jefferson, and Benjamin Franklin. At Adams's suggestion, Jefferson drafted the declaration, and although Congress made a number of changes, the Declaration of Independence reflects the thought of its principal authors. Later, Jefferson insisted that he never tried to be original, and that the document reflected the "mind" of the American people.

When Americans today read the declaration, they focus on the ideals of government set forth in the second paragraph: "life, liberty, and the pursuit of happiness." They tend to gloss over the long list of abuses charged against the king. But for Americans at the time, that indictment was the principle justification for the radical step of independence. Among other things, the king was charged with denying constitutional government to the colonists by interfering with the lawful work of the colonial assemblies, with denying the colonial merchants with access to ports, with allowing Parliament to tax the colonists without representation, and, worst of all, with armed invasion of the colonies. There is no mention of religion in the articles of indictment. Rather, the grievances centered on political and economic concerns. The charges constituted the heart of the case that Jefferson made before the court of world opinion. To gain support from France, a monarchy, American colonists needed to show that they were not opposing monarchy itself, but a rogue monarch who had violated the rights of his own subjects.

Despite the secular character of the charges, Eidsmoe and Barton insist that the declaration reflects Puritan and

Calvinist ideas rather than Enlightenment principles. For example, they note correctly that there are four references to God. While that is true, the designations are not those of the Christian God that the Puritans invoked; rather, they are deist constructions such as "nature's God." There is no mention of Christ or Savior or God the Father. Further, the Christian Right "historians" claim that the declaration contains a Puritan-inspired covenant, not a secular Lockean social contract. A comparison of the Puritan covenant of 1629 and the declaration of 1776 clarifies the question. The Puritan covenant was produced by God; it was God, Winthrop insisted, who endorsed the Christian commonwealth, and it was God who promised to bless it as long as the people were obedient, but would withdraw His blessing if they were disobedient. By contrast, "the governed," or "the people," drew up the social contract of the Declaration of Independence, and the governed, not God, maintain the right to determine their own form of government. Furthermore, the people alone decide when to abolish one government and institute a new one. While declaring that they enjoy "natural rights" from the Creator, Americans insisted that they would govern their own affairs on earth.

The most direct inspiration for Jefferson in drafting the Declaration of Independence was John Locke, the Scottish moral philosophers—Francis Hutcheson, Thomas Reid, James Beattie, and Dugald Stewart—and William Wollaston, the author of *The Religion of Nature Delineated*. John Eidsmoe argues that because of John Witherspoon's presence in the Congress, the declaration was also shaped by John Calvin and Calvinism. While Witherspoon was a Calvinist theologian, he was also a student of the Scottish Enlightenment. As president of the College of New Jersey, Witherspoon introduced to the students at Princeton "the latest discoveries in philosophy," including most specifically the teachings of Scottish Common Sense and Realism. From 1769–1771, James Madison was a student at Princeton under Witherspoon's presidency, when the college was a "cradle of liberty." A decade before Madison's matriculation, "religion held the dominant place in the minds and hearts of faculty and students." But political protest in the 1760s soon changed the character of the college. Undergraduates gathered in Nassau Hall to discuss the "injustice of the Stamp Act." Further, after the mid-1760s, commencements became occasions for "harangues on patriotism, or debates on the thesis that 'all men are free by the law of nature.'" John Witherspoon added his fervor to the Whig cause when he assumed the presidency in 1768. As a delegate to the Continental Convention, Witherspoon demonstrated his understanding of history in speaking out for republican government under a confederation of the states. In a 30 July 1776 debate, for instance, he argued against a proposal that small states pay the same amount of taxes as the large states. He commented, "We all agree that there must and shall be a confederation, for this war." But, he added, the proposal of equal taxation "will diminish the glory of our object, and depreciate our hope; it will damp the ardor of the people. The greatest danger we have, is of disunion among ourselves. Is it not plausible that the small States will be oppressed by the great ones? The Spartans and Helotes. The Romans and their dependents. Every Colony is a distinct person." Thus he understood that the central goal was political union to combat British tyranny. He was the only minister to sign the Declaration of Independence, in part because he understood that the question of independence was a political and not a theological issue. That was not the case with Presbyterian minister John Zubly of Georgia, who was a delegate to

Congress in 1775. His politics and theology made him unpopular among the other delegates. Early in his tenure he announced, "I came here with two views; one, to secure the rights of America; second, a reconciliation with Great Britain." And he was outspoken in opposition to republican government, stating at one point, "A republican government is little better than government of devils." A Calvinist, Zubly thought that the question of American independence was a matter of theology, not politics. He wanted Congress to focus on making America a Christian nation, not an independent state. He believed that God's grace, not human laws, was the ultimate solution. He thought it an "extreme absurdity" to struggle for "civil liberty, yet continue slaves to sin and lust." Through such preaching, Zubly made himself irrelevant in Congress. John Adams noted that Zubly was "the first Gentleman of the Cloth who has appeared in Congress," quickly adding, "I cannot but wish he may be the last."[27]

He was not the last, however, but John Witherspoon understood that the issue before Congress was not "sin and lust," but the unconstitutional acts of Parliament. The question was one of civil liberty: would Americans enjoy equal constitutional rights as the king's subjects residing in England? Moreover, he understood that civil liberty and religious liberty were interlinked. Again drawing on his knowledge of history, he noted, "There is not a single instance in history in which civil liberty was lost, and religious liberty preserved entire."[28] Unlike Zubly, Witherspoon believed that republican government was the surest safeguard of both civil and religious liberty.

---

[27] See Jim Schmidt, "The Reverend John Joachim Zubly's 'The Law of Liberty' Sermon: Calvinist Opposition to the American Revolution," *Georgia Historical Quarterly* 82 (Summer 1998): 354.

[28] Cited in ibid., 368.

It was not Calvinist theology but natural religion that inspired Jefferson's memorable phrase, the "pursuit of happiness." John Locke had used the phrase, but Jefferson also encountered it in Wollaston's *The Religion of Nature Delineated* (1759). Wollaston's central premise was that "Truth is but a conformity to nature: and to follow nature cannot be to combat truth." Truth is revealed in the "books of nature," which were written by the "Author of nature." Humans, through the right use of their reason, can discern God's truth from nature, and, conversely, "To deny things to be as they are is a transgression of the great law of our nature, the law of reason. For truth cannot be opposed, but reason must be violated." Wollaston qualified his confidence in reason, stating that "everyone pretends that his reason is right." Only that reason grounded in fair and accurate observation and experimentation into how things work reveals the truth. He also defined religion: "By religion I mean nothing else but an obligation to do (under which word I comprehend acts both of body and mind. I say, to do) what ought not to be omitted, and to forbear what ought not to be done." It is from this natural religion that Wollaston makes his case for the pursuit of happiness, and like Locke, he sees happiness as the end goal of human beings. To him, happiness is the result when the sum of pleasure exceeds the sum of pain, and, therefore, "To make itself happy is a duty, which every being, in proportion to its capacity, owes to itself."[29] Thus, the pursuit of happiness, as Jefferson understood it from Wollaston, is a natural right that government ought to protect.

History gets in the way of the Christian Right "historians." Their perspective is a theological hope, not a

---

[29] William Wollaston, *The Religion of Nature Delineated*, 7th ed. (Glasgow, 1746) 20, 37, 41, 53ff.

historical reality. They want America to be a Christian nation, so they read that hope back into the nation's founding. But history is about particular people at particular times doing particular things. And in 1776, the authors of the Declaration of Independence had a particular view of the world, an Enlightenment view, that is manifest in the document. Moreover, the self-styled "historians" fail to account for change over time, the essence of history. They are correct in seeing the stamp of Calvinism on the Puritan documents, but they fail to account for 150 years of change between when the "Puritan" fathers created a Christian commonwealth and when the "Founding" fathers declared independence and called for republican government. Much had happened in the intervening years, including the Great Awakening and Enlightenment, changes that altered institutions at every level of society. At Harvard, for example, by the birth of the United States more lawyers than ministers were being graduated each year. Religious uniformity was the ideal in 1629; religious diversity was the reality of 1776. In Puritan Massachusetts, conformity was demanded; in independent United States, individual freedom and choice were valued.

By conflating the sacred and the secular, the Christian Right confuses the respective messages of the ideals expressed in the Bible and in the Declaration of Independence. The biblical claim is that God is Creator and Ruler of all for all time and that the ultimate goal for all people should be a place in the Kingdom of God. It is not the "People's Republic of God," but the Kingdom of God. God, not "the people," define who is admitted and under what conditions. It is a covenanted kingdom. By contrast, the republic declared by the Declaration of Independence does not address the Kingdom of God, although many, if not most, Americans subscribed to that concept. Rather, it focuses on the immediate circumstances facing the colonists. For more than a decade, Americans had resisted the new imperial measures imposed by the British after the French and Indian War ended in 1763. Moreover, some colonists were eyeing the lands to the West as the future basis of what historian Marc Engel called a "mighty empire," an American, not a British, empire. Thus, they came to the point that the best way to get out from under oppressive British rule and to realize their own dreams for the future was to sever all ties with Britain. What happened in 1776 was just as electrifying as the arrival of Whitefield or the invention of Franklin's lightning rod a quarter century earlier. And one cannot understand 1776 without understanding the influence of the Great Awakening and Enlightenment on Americans' thinking. Both emboldened them to place the individual and individual experience above all other forms of earthly authority. While Awakened and Enlightened individuals disagreed, sometimes vehemently, on the particulars of their beliefs, both saw freedom and independence as natural, God-given rights, and it was upon that foundation that Americans created a new republic.

4

Constituting Religion in the
Newly Independent States

Thomas Jefferson and John Leland had similar ideas about the separation of church and state, although they used different metaphors to illustrate their respective positions. Inspired by Enlightenment ideas of free enquiry, Jefferson used his reason to argue that government ought to have nothing to do with religious matters other than to guarantee religious liberty. He assumed the leadership in Virginia's fight for religious liberty from 1776 to 1785, culminating in the Statute for Religious Freedom that he authored. Expressing his views in his *Notes on the State of Virginia* (1785), he argued that government had no more to do with religious beliefs than with the laws of physics. Reciting the case of Galileo, whose heliocentric views were denounced by the Catholic Church as being counter to Scripture, Jefferson wrote, "Government is just as infallible too when it fixes systems in physics. Galileo was sent to the inquisition for affirming that the earth was a sphere: the government had declared it to be as flat as a trencher, and Galileo was obliged to abjure his error."[1] To Jefferson, both religion and physics were beyond governmental influence.

---

[1] Thomas Jefferson, *Notes on the State of Virginia* (Paris, 1784–1785) 293.

John Leland agreed, but he substituted mathematics for physics to make his case. An evangelical minister from Massachusetts who itinerated in Virginia at the time of the fight for religious freedom, Leland played a major role in securing the triumph of Jefferson's bill calling for disestablishment and unfettered religious liberty. In his sermon *The Rights of Conscience Inalienable* (1791), Leland echoed Jefferson's argument:

> Is conformity of sentiments in matters of religion essential to the happiness of civil government? Not at all. Government has no more to do with the religious opinions of men than it has with the principles of the mathematics. Let every man speak freely without fear—maintain the principles that he believes—worship according to his own faith, either one God, three Gods, no God, or twenty Gods; and let government protect him in so doing.[2]

While Jefferson and Leland viewed the question from different worldviews, nonetheless, they agreed that separation of church and state was essential to religious liberty.

The fight for separation of church and state began in the states, a fight that cannot be understood outside the context of independence and individual rights. Evangelicals joined Enlightenment thinkers in the struggle. The question was not one of the *importance* of religion in the new states; rather it was the *place* of religion in them, a distinction often lost on today's Christian Right. While delegates in most of the state constitutional conventions thought that religion in general and Christianity in particular were important to their states, they did not think that the government should establish, support, or regulate it. Thus, with the notable

---

[2] John Leland, *The Rights of Conscience Inalienable* (New London CT: T. Green and Son, 1791) 13.

exceptions of Massachusetts and Connecticut, all the states thought the place of religion was in the hands of individuals, not in those of the state.

It is not surprising, then, that Leland fought for disestablishment in Massachusetts and Connecticut, arguing for the adoption of the Virginia model. Not all agreed with him. Like the Christian Right today, there were those who wanted close ties between the government and religion. One such person was Phillips Payson, a Congregational Minister in Chelsea, Massachusetts, who believed that religion was so important to civil order that the state must provide for its support. In his Election Day sermon delivered in 1778, he voiced the views of those who believed that only state coercion could put religion on a secure footing. The alternative of relying on voluntary contributions of church members was too uncertain. Payson based his argument for state-supported religion on the importance of religion: "the importance of religion to civil society and government is great indeed...the fear and reverence of God and the terrors of eternity, are the most powerful restraints on the minds of men...let the restraints of religion once be broken down...and one might well defy all human wisdom and power to support and preserve order and government in the state."[3]

Taking the contrary position, Isaac Backus, a leader of New England Baptists, vehemently opposed any form of state-supported religion. Baptists opposed a religious establishment based on their reading of the New Testament and on their reading of church history, which provided numerous examples of how state support of religion, while

---

[3] Phillips Payson, *Sermon Preached Before the Honorable Council and the Honorable House of Representatives of the State of Massachusetts-Bay, New-England, at Boston, on May 27, 1778* (Boston: John Gill, 1778).

perhaps beneficial to the favored group in the short term, in the long term corrupted the established church as the line blurred between what was in the state's interest and what was in the church's. Like Payson, Backus believed that religion served a vital role in civil society because religion provided moral instruction, and morality was essential for honest dealings in the marketplace and for citizen obedience to just laws. However, Backus and the Baptists believed that the best way for the state to assure the vitality of religion was to put it on a voluntary basis, that is, to leave it alone and let church members run and finance their own congregations. Baptists, along with Presbyterians and Methodists, were, on the eve of American independence, the fastest growing churches in British North America. They were convinced that the spirit of the Great Awakening, which had given a spur to evangelical churches, would continue and that, if left alone, evangelical churches would become dominant in the new republic.

Payson and Backus gave voice to the choices facing delegates to the Massachusetts Constitutional Convention: secure religion through state support or through the voluntary contributions of church members. A disinterested third party could see strengths and weaknesses in each position. If religion was to be state supported, it would be put on a solid financial foundation with taxes levied on and collected from all ratepayers. But, what would be the status of dissenters, those who did not subscribe to the established church? Payson and others who supported an establishment also favored religious toleration, that is, government granting the right of dissenters to worship as they please and even allot their share of taxes to their dissenting congregations. If religion was, on the other hand, made voluntary, religious freedom would be assured as individuals would decide which church, if any, to support.

But, would enough citizens voluntarily support religion to ensure that its influence would permeate all of society?

The same questions posed in Massachusetts were debated in all of the states as each wrestled with the place and role and support of religion. A decade before delegates to the Federal Convention in Philadelphia would decide the same issues at the federal level, delegates to state constitutional conventions struggled with them. This chapter examines that struggle, first by looking at Massachusetts, second by focusing on Virginia, and third by exploring the contagion of religious freedom that led to the disestablishment of religion in all the states.

State-Supported Religion and Religious Toleration in Massachusetts

In 1776, anticipating independence from Britain, the Continental Congress directed the colonies to draft republican constitutions. In addition to deciding on a structure of government and on the powers to grant that government, delegates to the state constitutional conventions were faced with the question of how to constitute religion. Involved were questions regarding establishment, religious freedom, and religious tests for officeholders.

Massachusetts was the scene of a contentious battle over the drafting and ratification of a constitution, in part because of religious disputes. Indeed, it took from 1778 to 1780 to secure ratification. Throughout its colonial history, Massachusetts had had a religious establishment, that is, state support of a particular church, specifically the Congregational churches. However, since the 1740s when the Great Awakening swept through the colony, there were a growing number of dissenters. Some were New Light Congregationalists, churches organized by evangelicals

146

who made a new birth experience the criterion for membership. In some cases, these New Lights had replaced an "unconverted" minister with an evangelical one of their choosing. In other instances, newborn evangelicals had separated themselves from their old congregations and established Separate Baptist churches. Thus, the much desired religious uniformity that had been sought at the colony's founding had been replaced by diversity. Furthermore, dissenters chafed under the establishment laws and sought freedom of religion, not the religious toleration that the legislature granted them.

Most Congregationalists advocated continuation of the colonial religious settlement, one that provided for ordered freedom. They cherished individual liberty as evidenced by their fight against British infringements on them, but at the same time they wanted a society of law and order. Religious debate threatened social harmony, so they thought it best to have one established religion while tolerating dissenters. Reverend Samuel West, Congregational minister at Dartmouth, was one of the combatants in a newspaper war fought over the religious question. Writing as "Irenaeus" in the 27 November 1780 edition of the *Boston Gazette and the Country Journal*, he argued for state-supported religion because he believed that submission to religious authority made better citizens. With its "doctrine of a future state of reward and punishment," religion is indispensable for maintaining social order because it provides a greater incentive for obedience to the law than do civil punishments."[4] Religion, then, was a handmaiden to government, and therefore its support must be guaranteed by the state and not left to the voluntary contributions of believers.

---

[4] *The Boston Gazette and the Country Journal*, 27 November 1780.

For Baptists, however, no argument for state support of religion was convincing. Isaac Backus urged the people of Massachusetts to learn from history lessons of how state support, while in the short term seemingly advantageous to Christians, turned out to be a Faustian bargain. He reminded readers of the plight of Christians in fourth-century Rome, who, after centuries of persecution, accepted Constantine's protection when granted Christianity special favor after he underwent a dramatic conversion to the faith. Speaking of Christ's founding of the Christian Church within the hostile Roman Empire, Backus wrote, "Now 'tis well known that this glorious Head made no use of secular force in the first setting up of the Gospel Church, when it might seem to be peculiarly needful if ever." But after Christ's death, some of his followers who suffered persecution began to think that state support would be a good thing and would promote the faith. So, Backus explained, "they moved Constantine, a secular prince, to draw his sword against heretics." Now Christians were the protected sect, and their persecutors were the dissenters. But, Backus warned, "earthly states are changeable, [and] the same sword that Constantine drew against heretics, Julian turned against the orthodox."[5] His message was clear: Christians should rely solely upon their God, who is the same always, rather than upon the state, which flutters with the political winds.

Backus also drew upon recent history to make his case for religious freedom. In 1778, he published a treatise, *Government and Liberty Described; and Ecclesiastical Tyranny Exposed.* For years Massachusetts had been the center of the

---

[5] Isaac Backus, *An Appeal to the Public for Religious Liberty*, vol. 1, in *Political Sermons of the American Founding Era.* 2 vols, Foreword by Ellis Sandoz, 2nd ed. (Indianapolis: Liberty Fund, 1998) I, 338.

fight against the "tyranny" of George III and Parliament. Using the language of Whigs to describe their plight, Patriots characterized the conflict as one between virtuous liberty on the side of the colonists and vicious tyranny on the side of the British. Similarly, Backus portrayed the fight for religious freedom. Those supporting complete religious freedom were virtuous; those advocating state-supported religion were vicious. The biblical text for his sermon was Galatians 5:1: "Stand fast therefore in the Liberty wherewith Christ hath made us free, and be not entangled again with the yoke of bondage." When Christians turn away from Christ and seek security in the state, they lose their freedom, because when the state grants a right, the state retains control over the extent and use of that right. To make his point, Backus cited a recent instance when the British government sought to support, and therefore control, religion in America. Eleven years earlier, the episcopal clergy in the colonies beseeched the Archbishop of Canterbury to send bishops to America. While the clergy seeking bishops claimed that all they wanted was to complete the organization of their church and not to infringe upon the religious liberty of non-Anglicans, Massachusetts Congregationalists were quick to protest. Leading the response was Charles Chauncey, an Old Light Boston minister. Backus quoted Chauncey as writing: "We are, in principle, against all civil establishments in religion. It does not appear to us, that God has entrusted the state with a right to make religious establishments. If the state in England has this delegated authority, must it not be owned, that the state in China, in Turkey, in Spain, has this authority likewise?" Backus argued that if Chauncey was right, then his indictment of civil establishments of religion still applied in Massachusetts. The new state had no more right to establish the Congregational churches there than did Britain or China or Turkey or Spain to establish their respective state-supported religions.[6]

Backus's arguments, however, failed to convince a majority of the delegates, and Massachusetts opted for a civil establishment of religion. The Constitution as ratified in 1780 did more than grant power to the state over religion; it recognized the importance of religion in civil society. The Preamble was just the sort of acknowledgment of God's importance to the state that William Williams had hoped to see in the United States Constitution:

> We, therefore, the people of Massachusetts, acknowledging, with grateful hearts, the goodness of the great Legislator of the universe, in affording us, in the course of His providence, an opportunity, deliberately and peaceably, without fraud, violence, or surprise, of entering into an original, explicit, and solemn compact with each other, and of forming a new constitution of civil government for ourselves and posterity; and devoutly imploring His direction in so interesting a design, do agree upon, ordain, and establish the following declaration of rights and frame of government as the constitution of the commonwealth of Massachusetts.[7]

While the designation for God, "the great Legislator of the universe," was more of a deist than a Christian phrase, nonetheless, it was an overt acknowledgment that the government rested under divine law.

Article II set forth the importance of religion in civil society, characterizing it as both a right and a duty:

---

[6] Isaac Backus, *Government and Liberty Described, and Ecclesiastical Tyranny Exposed* (Boston: Powars and Willis, 1778) 4–5.

[7] Massachusetts Constitution of 1780 found in Oscar and Mary Handlin, eds *The Popular Sources of Political Authority: Documents on the Massachusetts Constitution of 1780* (Cambridge MA: Belknap Press, 1966) 445–472.

It is the right as well as the duty of all men in society, publicly and at stated seasons, to worship the Supreme Being, the great Creator and Preserver of the universe. And no subject shall be hurt, molested, or restrained, in his person, liberty, or estate, for worshipping God in the manner and season most agreeable to the dictates of his own conscience, or for his religious profession or sentiments, provided he doth not disturb the public peace or obstruct others in their religious worship.

Strongly influenced by John Adams, the wording again reflects language more akin to that of natural theology than of the Christian faith. Instead of the "Lord Jesus Christ" or "Christ our Savior," the divine is referred to as "the Supreme Being, the great Creator and Preserver of the universe."[8]

If the Constitution said no more about religion than it did in the Preamble and Article II, one could make the case that religion was in the hands of the people and not in those of the state. But Article III made the Legislature the instrument of providing and supporting religious instruction. It reads:

Therefore, To promote their happiness and to secure the good order and preservation of their government, the people of this commonwealth have a right to invest their legislature with power to authorize and require, and the legislature shall, from time to time, authorize and require, the several towns, parishes, precincts, and other bodies-politic or religious societies to make suitable provision, at their own expense, for the institution of the public worship of God and for the support and maintenance of public Protestant teachers of piety, religion, and morality in all cases where such provision shall not be made voluntarily.[9]

---

[8] Ibid.
[9] Ibid.

The Legislature had power to mandate institutions for public worship in towns and parishes, and in case the local jurisdictions failed in that duty, the Legislature retained the power to institute acceptable places of worship. Thus, the state had a direct voice in religion. If necessary, the state could intervene in local affairs and decide what is, for example, an "orthodox" church. Further, Article III granted the state coercive powers over church attendance: "And the people of this commonwealth have also a right to, and do, invest their legislature with authority to enjoin upon all the subjects an attendance upon the instructions of the public teachers aforesaid, at stated times and seasons, if there be any on whose instructions they can conscientiously and conveniently attend." The Constitution did contain a provision that revenue from the state-levied tithe would be apportioned according to the taxpayers' religious preferences:

> And all moneys paid by the subject to the support of public worship and of public teachers aforesaid shall, if he require it, be uniformly applied to the support of the public teacher or teachers of his own religious sect or denomination, provided there be any on whose instructions he attends; otherwise it may be paid toward the support of the teacher or teachers of the parish or precinct in which the said moneys are raised.[10]

However, in towns and parishes without dissenting congregations, all tithes went to the established church.

Finally, the Massachusetts constitution tied one's religious beliefs to his civil liberties. Officeholders must submit to a religious test to ensure their orthodoxy. The statement was succinct. Upon taking office, the person must swear: "I, A.B., do declare that I believe the Christian

---

[10] Ibid.

religion, and have a firm persuasion of its truth." Thus, only confessing Christians could hold office.

The constitution of adjoining Connecticut also reflected that state's Puritan heritage. The legislature decided to continue governing under its colonial constitution, the *Fundamental Orders of Connecticut* (1639), and it was not until 1818 that Connecticut drafted a new state constitution. The *Fundamental Orders* recognized "the word of God" as the authority of civil government whose end was "peace and union," and whose means was "an orderly and decent Government established according to God." Churches were mandated "to maintain and preserve the liberty and purity of the Gospel of our Lord Jesus which we now profess, as also, the discipline of the Churches, which according to the truth of the said Gospel is now practiced amongst us." And civil government was to follow the same course of discipline and unity: "as also in our civil affairs to be guided and governed according to such Laws, Rules, Orders, and Decrees as shall be made, ordered, and decreed."[11]

In 1708, some of the more Conservative ministers of Connecticut's Congregational Churches were concerned about the lack of discipline and disunity that they saw spreading throughout the colony. Like religion in neighboring Massachusetts, there seemed to these clergymen to be a general decline in religious fervor, a falling off in the zeal manifested by the earliest settlers. To re-instill discipline and unity in the congregations, a synod

---

[11] The Fundamental Orders of Connecticut found in *The Federal and State Constitutions Colonial Charters, and Other Organic Laws of the States, Territories, and Colonies Now or Heretofore Forming the United States of America,* compiled and edited Under the Act of Congress of 30 June 1906 by Francis Newton Thorpe (Washington, D.C.: Government Printing Office, 1909) 252–249.

met at Saybrook and drew up a new church constitution consisting of fifteen articles, which became known as the Saybrook Platform or, as it is sometimes referred to, the Standing Order. The Saybrook assembly adopted the Calvinist-inspired Westminster Confession (1643) as its doctrinal statement, and it created a consociation of congregations, or Presbyterian, form of church government. Both the creed and the government were incorporated to ensure a more disciplined faith in several churches. Teachings must conform to the Westminster Confession, and discipline was enforced by presbyters, which were governing bodies of ministers and laymen that had the power to censure local churches.

While ten of the thirteen states emerged from colonies that had had some sort of religious establishment, only Massachusetts and Connecticut persisted with establishments. Other states moved toward greater toleration, although none went as far toward religious freedom as did Pennsylvania. As a colony, Pennsylvania had welcomed Protestants of all confessions and soon became the most religiously diverse colony in British North America. That background was reflected in the declaration of rights that prefaced the state's first constitution:

> That all men have a natural and unalienable right to worship Almighty God according to the dictates of their own consciences and understanding: And that no man ought or of right can be compelled to attend any religious worship, or erect or support any place of worship, or maintain any ministry, contrary to, or against, his own free will and consent: Nor can any man, who acknowledges the being of a God, be justly deprived or abridged of any civil right as a citizen, on account of his religious sentiments or peculiar mode of religious worship: And that no authority can or ought to be vested in, or assumed by any power whatever, that shall in any case interfere with, or in any

manner controul, the right of conscience in the free exercise of religious worship.[12]

South Carolina in 1778 adopted a constitution that granted toleration but established Protestant Christianity in general, rather than a particular denomination. It read, "That all persons and religious societies who acknowledge that there is one God, and a future state of rewards and punishments, and that God is publicly to be worshipped, shall be freely tolerated. The Christian Protestant religion shall be deemed, and is hereby constituted and declared to be, the established religion of this State."[13] While no other state adopted any type of religious establishment, most stopped short of complete religious freedom. They continued to link religious affiliation and civil rights, especially through religious tests for officeholders. A couple examples will suffice. The North Carolina Constitution of 1776 contained the following religious test: "That no person, who shall deny the being of God or the truth of the Protestant religion, or the divine authority either of the Old or New Testaments, or who shall hold religious principles incompatible with the freedom and safety of the State, shall be capable of holding any office or place of trust or profit in the civil department within this State."[14] The Maryland constitution adopted in 1776 stated, "That no other test or qualification ought to be required, on admission to any office of trust or profit, than such oath of support and fidelity to this State, and such oath of office, as shall be directed by this Convention or the Legislature of this State, and a declaration of a belief in the Christian religion."[15]

---

[12] The Pennsylvania Constitution of 1776 found in Thorpe, *The Federal and State Constitutions.*

[13] The South Carolina Constitution of 1778 found in ibid.

[14] The North Carolina Constitution of 1776 found in ibid.

[15] The Maryland Constitution of 1776 found in ibid.

Voluntary Religion and Religious Liberty in Virginia

No state wrestled more with the question of the place of religion than did Virginia. In 1776, the General Assembly began the task of drafting a constitution, and religion quickly emerged as a contentious issue. The matter was put aside for much of the Revolutionary War. After resuming deliberations after the war, the question of establishment persisted to vex the legislators. It was not until 1785 that the matter was finally resolved with the passage of the Virginia Statute for Religious Freedom.

To understand the debate in Virginia, one needs to understand the religious makeup of the state during its colonial period and how it had changed by 1776. While the Church of England was established in early colonial Virginia, the colony was never as monolithic as its establishment would suggest. Indeed, before separating from England in 1776, Virginia was characterized by three religious groups, all professing to be Christians, but each highly suspicious of the others. First, there was the Church of England, transplanted into the Virginia wilderness from the colony's early settlement. The colony's charter included a religious mission: to declare the "Christian religion to such people, as yet live in darkness and miserable ignorance of the true knowledge and worship of God." Though the "ignorant" meant Native Americans, no doubt royal officials also had in mind some of the poor English subjects who would settle the land. The important thing was for the settlers to plant "true" Christianity in the colony, and that meant Christianity as expressed by the Church of England. So successful was the transplantation that, by 1612, the colony's "Lawes," equating Christianity with the Church of England, proclaimed Virginia a "Christian Colonie." Further, to some it was a chosen land.

According to John Rolfe, noted more for promoting tobacco cultivation than theological orthodoxy, Virginians were a "peculiar people, marked and chosen by the finger of God."[16]

Virginia's Church of England was, first of all, Protestant. Being Protestant meant that it was vehemently opposed to the Roman Catholic Church, and the colony's historical texts are replete with pejorative epithets hurled at Catholics, such as "Papists" and "Romanists." The Virginia Church adhered to such Protestant doctrines as "salvation by faith alone" and the sufficiency of Scripture for instruction unto salvation, but it soon evolved into a Latitudinarian sect that paid less attention to doctrinal hairsplitting and more to moral teaching.

In part, doctrine was downplayed because the Church in Virginia was deficient in much of the institutional scaffolding necessary for strict discipline. Indeed, Virginia's lack of ecclesiastical superstructure represents the greatest difference between church-state relations in the Old and the New World. In the Virginia wilderness there was no resident bishop, and there were no ecclesiastical courts. Virginia's churches fell under the jurisdiction of the Bishop of London, who delegated superintendence of the colonial Anglican church to commissaries. Missionaries of the Society for the Propagation of the Gospel (SPG) provided an additional bridge between England and Virginia, but, in fact, governance of the churches rested primarily with local vestries made up of the planting gentry, who also dominated local and provincial politics. It was they who claimed and exercised the power to invest and remove clergymen, giving the laity powers unimagined in England.

---

[16] See Darrett Rutman, *American Puritanism: Faith and Practice* (New York: Lippincott, 1979) 4–5, 37–38.

From early settlement, the Church of England was the established church. Establishment meant that the Church received state tax revenues to build and maintain parishes and to support ministers. In 1632, the House of Burgesses passed a law requiring that there be a "uniformitie throughout this colony both in substance and circumstance to the cannons and constitution of the Church of England." While Non-Conformists enjoyed freedom of conscience, such freedom extended only to private thoughts and utterances. In public, all Virginians were expected to support the official church, and all were taxed for its benefit. The government exercised its police powers to punish those who blasphemed the Church or its leaders and those "heretics" who openly avowed teachings at odds with those in the Church's official articles of faith. Further, the legislature decided whether or not a sect would be granted glebe lands, and it dictated that dissenters must provide their own financing to support their ministers while continuing to pay taxes to support the Anglican priests in their parish.

By the middle of the eighteenth century, Virginia's second group of Christians made their presence known. They were the evangelicals. Evangelicals were Protestants who distinguished themselves by adhering to a specific set of beliefs that, according to historian David Bebbington, includes biblicism, a particular regard for the Bible (e.g., all spiritual truth is to be found in its pages); crucicentrism, a focus on the atoning work of Christ on the cross; conversionism, the belief that human beings need to be converted; and, activism, the belief that the Gospel needs to be expressed in effort. During the Great Awakening, the evangelical revivals of the 1740s, evangelicals added a fifth distinction: a dramatically new emphasis on the role of the Holy Spirit in conversion, especially as manifested in periodic revivals, defined as special seasons of God's outpouring of grace. Presbyterians, Methodists, and Baptists began flowing into Virginia in the mid-1740s, settling primarily in the Piedmont along the frontier. By 1776, evangelical churches, collectively, constituted the majority and fastest growing religious group in Virginia, although each sect remained a minority.

The third group consisted of a small but influential body of persons who were variously referred to as Christian rationalists, deists, devotees of natural religion, or freethinkers. Some of Virginia's leading public figures fell into this category, including most notably Thomas Jefferson, James Madison, George Mason, and George Washington. All regarded themselves as religious and even Christian, but they insisted on defining for themselves what "Christian" meant. Further, they regarded human reason as central to understanding how nature and society worked. Moreover, they thought that religious claims, including those contained within the Bible and deemed to be divine revelation, must be subjected to the test of reason. Finally, they had little use for the theological squabbling among sectarians, believing instead that morality was far more important than orthodox teachings.

While Virginians debated the question of church-state relations in the period spanning 1776 to 1785, the three religious groups adhered to different conceptions of what it meant to be a Christian, making it difficult to agree on a single conception and helping explain why Henry's proposal to insert the name of Christ failed. Anglicans believed that a Christian was one who subscribed to the Thirty-Nine Articles of the Church that set forth its fundamental beliefs. From 1689, believers had expressed their faith by swearing: "I do willingly and from my heart subscribe to the Thirty-Nine Articles of Religion of the

United Church of England and Ireland." Evangelicals, especially those influenced by the Great Awakening, maintained that only those who had experienced a spiritual "New Birth" could claim to be Christian. They insisted that good works were of no avail in salvation, including that of subscribing to creeds and articles of faith. Only the Indwelling Christ could bring the convert from the darkness of sin to the light of grace. Freethinkers refused to allow any church or creed to define what it meant to be a Christian, and they were skeptical of emotion-laden conversion experiences. In a 1789 letter, Jefferson wrote, "I never submitted the whole system of my opinions to the creed of any party of men whatever in religion, in philosophy, in politics, or in anything else where I was capable of thinking for myself. Such an addiction is the last degradation of a free and moral agent."[17] All religious truth-claims, he insisted, must be brought before the seat of reason for validation.

Virginians' civil liberties were directly related to their religious affiliations. Only members of the Church of England could hold public office. By a law of 1705, anyone denying the doctrine of the Trinity or stating that the Christian religion was not true or contending that the Scriptures were not of divine authority suffered greatly. On the first offense, the violator lost access to public office. On the second, he faced the prospects of his children being taken from him and placed in "more orthodox hands." In addition, he faced up to three years in prison. Thomas Jefferson asserted that these laws amounted to "religious slavery."[18] They also account for why he, as an unorthodox

---

[17] Peterson, *Thomas Jefferson: Writings*, 941.
[18] See Jefferson, *Notes on the State of Virginia*, 231.

officeholder, for the most part, kept his personal beliefs to himself.

Virginia dissenters suffered persecution for practicing their faith both before and after the Declaration of Independence. In comparison to religious persecution in Europe where thousands died for their faith, that in Virginia was for the most part bloodless and relatively mild. However, to those who deemed liberty of conscience to be a natural right, especially after the Declaration of Independence, any encroachment of their rights was a total breach. Baptists were the primary targets of religious persecution in Virginia, with Presbyterians being attacked as well. Members of the established Church of England were the persecutors, sometimes acting on their own as vigilantes and other times acting in concert with local officials. Baptists were sometimes singled out for physical violence because their censure of wealthy Anglicans for such behavior as drinking, swearing, and dancing incurred a level of animosity that transcended theological differences. In one notorious example of persecution, a popular Baptist preacher, "Swearin' Jack" Waller, illustrates how the attacks were aimed to humiliate as well as to inflict pain. A contemporary account told the story:

> The Parson of the Parish [accompanied by the local sheriff] would keep running the end of his horsewhip in [Waller's] mouth, laying his whip across the hymn book, etc. When done singing [Waller] proceeded to prayer. In it he was violently jerked off the stage; they caught him by the back part of his neck, beat his head against the ground, sometimes up and sometimes down, they carried him

through the gate...where a gentleman [the sheriff] gave him...twenty lashes with his horsewhip.[19]

As relations between the colonists and Britain deteriorated, James Madison worried about the effect of the persecution of dissenting evangelicals on their willingness to fight for independence and support the new republic. He had reason to worry about Baptist loyalty to Virginia because he knew firsthand about how Anglicans had attacked Baptists. After graduating from the College of New Jersey in 1771, he returned home and the following year witnessed and condemned the persecution of Baptist ministers in Orange and Culpeper Counties whose "offense" was preaching the Gospel without first obtaining state licenses mandated by law. The ministers recognized no authority for preaching the good news of Christ except that of divine revelation, and they refused to seek state permission. Many Baptist ministers refused to apply to local authorities for a license to preach, as Virginia law required, for they thought it intolerable to ask another man's permission to preach the Gospel. If they preached without a license, they were subject to arrest for "unlawfull Preaching," as was Nathaniel Saunders (1735–1808), minister of the Mountain Run Baptist Church in Orange County.[20] While Madison's beliefs were different from Saunders's, leaning more toward Enlightenment Rationalism than Baptist Calvinism, nonetheless, Madison agreed that no state can restrict the right of people to

---

[19] For the account of Waller's persecution, see the Library of Congress's online exhibit, "Religion and the Founding of the American Republic: Religion and the State Governments," at http://www.loc.gov/exhibits/religion/rel05.html (accessed 8 August 2012).

[20] See *Summons to Nathaniel Saunders*, 22 August 1772, Manuscript, Virginia Baptist Historical Society (140), Richmond VA.

worship according to the dictates of their consciences, and he gave legal representation to the Baptists. James Madison was not the only patriot to despair, as he did in 1774, that the "diabolical Hell conceived principle of persecution rages" in his native colony. Accordingly, civil libertarians like Madison and Thomas Jefferson joined Baptists and Presbyterians to defeat the campaign for state financial involvement in religion in Virginia.[21]

David Barrow, pastor of the Mill Swamp Baptist Church in the Portsmouth, Virginia, area, discovered that even as Virginians fought for natural rights, some of them continued to persecute dissenters. In 1778, Barrow and a "ministering brother," Edward Mintz, were attacked while conducting a service in 1778. According to a witness,

> As soon as the hymn was given out, a gang of well-dressed men came up to the stage...and sang one of their obscene songs. Then they took to plunge both of the preachers. They plunged Mr. Barrow twice, pressing him into the mud, holding him down, nearly succeeding in drowning him...His companion was plunged but once...Before these persecuted men could change their clothes they were dragged from the house, and driven off by these enraged churchmen.[22]

It was in the midst of this kind of persecution that Virginians took up the question of how to constitute religion in the state. On 8 November 1776, the clergy of the Church of England presented a memorial to the Virginia Assembly calling for a constitutional establishment of an episcopal church. With the War of Independence afoot,

---

[21] James Madison, letter to William Bradford, Jr., January 1774 in Hunt, ed., *The Writings of James Madison*, 1:21.

[22] For an account of Barrow's dunking and a painting depicting the scene, see http://www.loc.gov/exhibits/religion/rel05.html (accessed 8 August 2012).

Patriots regarded the Church of England as an agent of the enemy, thus it could not continue as the established church. However, many of the clergy who swore allegiance to the Patriot cause rushed to ensure the continuation of state support for religion. Sponsors of the memorial promised that the new establishment would not encroach upon "the Christian Rights of any sect or establishment of men." Nonetheless, they argued, a "religious establishment in a State is conducive to its peace and happiness," and "it, therefore, cannot be improper for the legislative body of a State to consider how such opinions as are most consonant to reason and of the best efficacy in human affairs may be propagated and supported." Moreover, they asserted, "the doctrines of Christianity have a greater tendency to produce virtue amongst men than any human laws or institutions," and "these can be best taught and preserved in their purity in an established church." As proof, they pointed to the 150 years of the Church's establishment in colonial Virginia, under which "order and internal tranquility, true piety and virtue have more prevailed than in most other parts of the world." They warned that disestablishment would result in religious chaos: "all denominations of Christians [would] be placed upon a level," leading to a competition among sects that would produce "much confusion, [and] probably civil commotions will attend the contest."[23]

Thomas Jefferson did not buy the argument. Instead, he asked the assembly to consider the experience of colonial Pennsylvania, where competing sects existed solely through the voluntary financial support of their members, and where religion had "long subsisted without any establishment at all." Moreover, he continued, the absence

---

[23] Charles James, ed., *Documentary History of the Struggle for Religious Liberty in Virginia* (New York: Da Capo Press, 1971) 76–77.

164

of state support in Pennsylvania did not result in the triumph of religious enthusiasm or other dangerous fanatical expressions. Rather, he wrote, "Religion is well supported; of various kinds, indeed, but all good enough; all sufficient to preserve peace and order; or if a sect arises, whose tenets would subvert morals, good sense has fair play, and reasons and laughs it out of doors, without suffering the State to be troubled with it."[24] What Jefferson described was a free marketplace of religion where all sects were able to compete without any state interference.

In 1777, Jefferson wrote a bill he cleverly titled, *A Bill for Establishing Religious Freedom.* Rather than establishing religion or a religion, his bill's purpose was to make a lawful establishment of religious freedom. He began with his view, influenced by John Locke's *Essay on Human Understanding,* of how the human mind operated: "the opinions and belief of men depend not on their own will, but follow involuntarily the evidence proposed to their minds." Jefferson added his belief "that Almighty God hath created the mind free, and manifested his supreme will that free it shall remain by making it altogether insusceptible of restraint." It followed from that premise "that all attempts to influence it by temporal punishments, or burthens, or by civil incapacitations, tend only to beget habits of hypocrisy and meanness, and are a departure from the plan of the holy author of our religion, who being lord both of body and mind, yet chose not to propagate it by coercions on either, as was in his Almighty power to do, but to extend it by its influence on reason alone." From that reasoning, Jefferson made his proposal:

> Be it therefore enacted by the General Assembly, That no man shall be compelled to frequent or support any

---

[24] Jefferson, *Notes on the State of Virginia,* 160–61.

religious worship, place, or ministry whatsoever, nor shall be enforced, restrained, molested, or burdened in his body or goods, nor shall otherwise suffer on account of his religious opinions or belief; but that all men shall be free to profess, and by argument to maintain, their opinions in matters of religion, and that the same shall in nowise diminish, enlarge, or affect their civil capacities.[25]

If passed, the bill would end religious establishment in Virginia and recognize complete religious freedom as a natural right that government cannot infringe upon but must protect.

After being introduced in 1779, Jefferson's bill was postponed after a second reading. In what could be considered a partial victory for those sympathetic with Jefferson's views, the assembly voted to deprive the Church of England clergymen the tax support they had long enjoyed. For the next five years, the matter was set aside as the war raged. Then in 1784, Patrick Henry sponsored a bill for a general religious assessment, which triggered a new round of debate over the place of religion in Virginia. The *Journal of the Virginia House of Delegates* for 24 December 1784 contains the wording of the bill in its final form:

Whereas the general diffusion of Christian knowledge hath a natural tendency to correct the morals of men, restrain their vices, and preserve the peace of society; which cannot be effected without a competent provision for learned teachers, who may be thereby enabled to devote their time and attention to the duty of instructing such citizens, as from their circumstances and want of education, cannot otherwise attain such knowledge; and it is judged that such

---

[25] As passed into law, Jefferson's bill became *An Act for Establishing Religious Freedom.* It was published as a broadside, a copy of which may be found as Thomas Jefferson. July 1786. Broadside. In the Rare Book and Special Collections Division, Library of Congress.

provision may be made by the Legislature, without counteracting the liberal principle heretofore adopted and intended to be preserved by abolishing all distinctions of pre-eminence amongst the different societies or communities of Christians.[26]

In the bill, Henry repeated the argument that the public support of religion is essential in a republic, which depends upon virtuous citizens to obey the law. At the same time, he provided for preservation of the "liberal principle" of religious liberty as stated in the Virginia Declaration of Rights, which stated "[t]hat religion, or the duty which we owe to our Creator, and the manner of discharging it, can be directed only by reason and conviction, not by force or violence; and therefore all men are equally entitled to the free exercise of religion, according to the dictates of conscience; and that it is the mutual duty of all to practice Christian forbearance, love, and charity toward each other."[27]

Some of Virginia's most influential leaders lined up in support of the general assessment bill. Richard Henry Lee, who had gained national notoriety when he moved in the Continental Congress on 7 June 1776 that the United States declare its independence from Britain, supported the bill, agreeing with Henry that religion was "the surest means of creating the virtuous citizens needed to make a republican government work." In a letter dated 26 November 1784 to James Madison, who opposed the measure, he commented, "refiners may weave as fine a web of reason as they please,

---

[26] *A Bill Establishing a Provision for Teachers of the Christian Religion,* Patrick Henry, Virginia House of Delegates, 24 December 1784. Broadside. Manuscript Division, Library of Congress.

[27] Ibid.

but the experience of all times shows religion to be the guardian of morals."[28]

In a letter dated 3 October 1785 to his friend and neighbor, George Mason, George Washington offered qualified support for the general assessment bill. On the one hand, he said that he did not oppose "making people pay towards the support of that which they profess." On the other, he thought it was unwise and "impolitic" to pass a law that would cause dissenters to protest and disturb public tranquility.[29]

The assembly received scores of petitions on both sides of the issue. A typical petition supporting the general assessment came from Surry County and is dated 14 November 1785. It reads in part:

> True Religion is most friendly to social and political Happiness—That a conscientious Regard to the approbation of Almighty God lays the most effectual restraint on the vicious passions of Mankind affords the most powerful incentive to the faithful discharge of every social Duty and is consequently the most solid Basis of private and public Virtue is a truth which has in some measure been acknowledged at every Period of Time and in every Corner of the Globe.[30]

The reference to "True Religion" illustrates that, then, as now, what is deemed as "true" is never transparent to all and is hotly contested. Christian Right "historians" fail to capture the contested nature of Christianity in American history and how any attempt to impose one expression has

---

[28] Richard Henry Lee to James Madison, 26 November 1784. Manuscript letter. Manuscript Division, Library of Congress.

[29] George Washington to George Mason, 3 October 1785. Manuscript copy, Letterbook, 1785–1786. Manuscript Division, Library of Congress.

[30] Petition to the Virginia General Assembly, from Surry County, Virginia, 14 November 1785. Manuscript. The Library of Virginia.

been opposed by those holding different beliefs. In this instance, although Henry's bill did not specify one particular sect, dissenters feared that the legislature would favor those of the episcopal ecclesiology over all others.

To counter Henry's bill, Baptists and Presbyterians flooded the assembly with petitions. Reaction from evangelicals was swift and largely negative. A group of Baptists voiced their disapproval of even a "Christian" establishment, arguing that it would give government a say in religious matters. "When legislatures undertake to pass laws about religion," they petitioned, "religion loses its form, and Christianity is reduced to a system of worldly policy."[31] Their concern was protecting religion from government. Madison had the opposite concern: protecting government from religion. Writing in the early 1800s, but reflecting sentiments he had expressed in 1785, he reflected on the question of a Christian establishment in America. He wrote, as "starkly guarded as is the separation between Religion and Government in the Constitution of the United States, the danger of encroachment by Ecclesiastical Bodies" had become evident as churches sought favors from government. He cited as an example a Kentucky law that exempted churches from taxation, arguing that religious groups were undermining the state's fiscal soundness.[32]

Though most evangelicals opposed the bill for a Christian establishment, the measure caused a rift in evangelical ranks when Presbyterians were tempted to support the bill, thinking that a general assessment would provide them with much-needed financial support. While Baptists remained adamant in their position that the state

---

[31] James, ed., *Documentary History*, 123.
[32] Jack Rakove, *James Madison: Writings* (New York: Library of America, 1999) 760.

had no role in the support of religion, some Presbyterian clergymen expressed their willingness to give the measure a chance. In considering the bill, the clergy from the Hanover Presbytery first lectured the assembly on the proper relation between church and state. The state's power, they maintained, extended only to temporal matters: "We conceive that human legislation ought to have human affairs alone for its concern." Government exists solely for the "preservation and happiness of society," and therefore its public cares should be confined to that end. All else is outside the sphere entrusted to statesmen, which means that citizens' thoughts, faith, worship, and confessions are "beyond their reach." In sum, "Religion...[is] a spiritual system, and its ministers in a professional capacity, ought not to be under the direction of the State." However, they concluded, if the state would support all religion without preference to a particular sect, then, the clergy declared, Presbyterians wanted to participate in that support.[33]

James Madison was appalled by the breach in the evangelical ranks. He noted that the "Episcopal" people, including the Methodists, were for the measure, and that the laity of the other sects opposed it, as did the clergy, except those from the Hanover Presbytery. He accused the Hanover clergymen of being opportunists. They were, he charged, "as ready to set up an establishment which is to take them in as they were to pull down that which shut them out." He declared, "I do not know a more shameful contrast than might be found between their memorials on the latter and former occasion."[34]

To Madison's delight, the clergymen soon reversed themselves on the question of a broad religious

---

[33] James, ed., *Documentary History*, 233–34.
[34] Ibid., 130.

establishment. Two influences seemed to sway them. First, Presbyterian laity disagreed with the clergy and opposed any government aid to religion. Evangelicals, especially Baptists and Presbyterians, were lay-led denominations, with congregations that did not hesitate to challenge their ministers, especially on social and political matters. Second, the clergy, either through pressure from the laity or from their own further reflection, grew "alarmed at the probability of farther interference of the Legislature, if they began to dictate in matters of religion."[35] If government has the power to support Presbyterians today, they reasoned, a future government might turn that power against the sect.

Supported by evangelicals that were once again united in the cause of separation, Thomas Jefferson introduced a bill calling for a ban on any religious establishment, no matter how broadly conceived. Baptists gave the bill their hearty support. Baptist pastor John Leland gave voice to the Baptist position that each individual stands before God and is answerable only to God for his or her religious choices. According to Leland, every man must give an account of himself to God, and therefore every man "ought to be at liberty to serve God in that way that he can best reconcile it to his conscience." He added that "religion is a matter between God and individuals: religious opinions of men not being the objects of civil government, nor any way under its control." Government funding of religion as proposed under the General Assessment Bill gave control to the state over religion. Leland understood that that which government finances, government to some measure regulates and controls. No one was more outspoken in support of complete separation of church and state. It was

---

[35] Cited in Loren Beth, *The American Theory of Church and State* (Gainesville FL: University of Florida Press, 1958) 64.

within that context that he declared that "government has no more to do with the religious opinions of men than it has with the principles of mathematics."[36] In a Fourth of July oration in 1802, Leland summarized views that he espoused in Virginia. He warned his listeners:

> Never promote men who seek after a state-established religion; it is spiritual tyranny—the worst of despotism. It is turnpiking the way to heaven by human law, in order to establish ministerial gates to collect toll. It converts religion into a principle of state policy..., and the gospel into merchandise. Heaven forbids the bans of marriage between church and state; their embraces therefore, must be unlawful. Guard against those men who make a great noise about religion, in choosing representatives. It is electioneering. If they knew the nature and worth of religion, they would not debauch it to such shameful purposes. If pure religion is the criterion to denominate candidates, those who make a noise about it must be rejected, for their wrangle about it, proves that they are void of it. Let honesty, talents, and quick despatch, characterise the men of your choice. Such men will have a sympathy with their constituents, and will be willing to come to the light, that their deeds may be examined....[37]

Before Jefferson's bill came to a vote, Henry made one last attempt to preserve a broadly stated establishment. He proposed inserting the name of "Jesus Christ" into the preamble of Jefferson's bill for religious freedom. Jefferson's draft referred to "the holy author of our religion." Henry proposed replacing Jefferson's deistic "holy author" with the explicitly Christian name "Jesus Christ." Besides its religious significance, the insertion was a shrewd political

---

[36] John Leland, *The Rights of Conscience Inalienable*, 7 and 13.

[37] L.F. Greene, ed., *The Writings of John Leland* (New York: Arno Press, 1969) 164. The 4th of July Oration is found on pages 260–70.

move. Who could object to adding the name of Christ to the document? Henry believed that Virginia, like all of the United States, was founded on Christian principles and that the assembly should acknowledge that heritage by mentioning the name of its divine author. Henry had once proposed the establishment of the Episcopal Church as the state's official, tax-supported religion, believing that religion was the fountainhead of moral instruction in a free nation and was too important to be left to voluntary contributions of church members. After witnessing the powerful opposition to the establishment of a particular Christian sect as violating the "liberal principle" that animated the new republic, he thought it wise for the state to support the "Christian Religion," not any particular sect, but Christianity in general. He believed that despite sectarian differences, all Christians could agree on a set of fundamental principles that would promote republican virtue. Surely, Henry thought, all Christians would approve of the insertion of the name "Jesus Christ" in the statute.[38]

James Madison immediately objected. Subscribing to a central tenet of John Locke's liberalism, Madison opposed any tyranny over the individual, including tyranny of the majority. He knew that, while most Virginians were Christians, the several sects disagreed with each other over basic assumptions of faith and practice. Further, he knew that each dissenting sect was a minority, and as such, feared the tyranny of a majority, which would surely exist, he thought, with the establishment of an official religion. So, he asked, what authority defined Christianity? Was it the Bible, and if so, which edition and what translation? Within

---

[38] For a contextualized account of the Henry-Madison debate, see Chris Beneke, *Beyond Toleration: The Religious Origins of American Pluralism* (Oxford: Oxford University Press, 2006) 163–64.

the Bible, which books were deemed to be canonical and which apocryphal? And whose interpretation of those sacred Scriptures should prevail: the Trinitarian's or the Unitarian's, the New Light's or the Old Light's, the Evangelical's or the Episcopalian's? Worse still, what would happen if Christians could not agree on what is Christian? Then the issue would become a government matter, and who in the government would determine what is properly "Christian"? Would it be the legislature or judges or magistrates?[39] To Madison, civil lawmakers should never legislate religious belief, which was a matter for a free conscience to decide. Legislators should confine themselves to guaranteeing religious liberty, not prescribing religious tenets.

After opposing Henry's proposal on the floor of the legislature, Madison wrote a treatise that remains as one of the most forceful arguments ever written for the separation of church and state. Titled, *A Memorial and Remonstrance Against Religious Assessments*, the document is a systematic defense of religious liberty drawn from Madison's extensive reading of history and political theory. He opened by asserting that religion is a natural right granted by the Creator and that, therefore, it "can be directed only by reason and conviction, not by force or violence." Moreover, he continued, "in matters of Religion, no man's right is abridged by the institution of Civil Society and that Religion is wholly exempt from its cognizance." Madison warned those who agreed with Henry that a Christian establishment is desirable: "the same authority which can establish Christianity, in exclusion of all other Religions, may establish with the same ease any particular sect of Christians, in exclusion of all other Sects." He likened state

---

[39] Ibid.

power over religion to Parliament's insistence on taxing Americans, arguing "that the same authority which can force a citizen to contribute three pence only of his property for the support of any one establishment, may force him to conform to any other establishment in all cases whatsoever." Henry's bill, Madison contended, rested on two fallacious assumptions. First, it implied "either that the Civil Magistrate is a competent Judge of Religious Truth; or that he may employ Religion as an engine of Civil policy." Madison reminded his readers that, throughout history, rulers have proven to be anything but competent in judging religious truth and that the use of religion to promote state policy is an "unhallowed perversion of the means of salvation." Second, Henry's bill, Madison averred, was unnecessary for the support of religion. Again, drawing on history, he wrote, "it is known that this Religion [Christianity] both existed and flourished, not only without the support of human laws, but in spite of every opposition from them, and not only during the period of miraculous aid, but long after it had been left to its own evidence and the ordinary care of Providence."[40]

Many from the Christian Right identify with Patrick Henry. By insisting, like Henry, that the United States is a Christian nation, they ignore how Henry's stance would have resulted in religious toleration but not religious freedom. Thus, they are indicted by the outcome of the struggle between Madison and Henry on the question of religious liberty: Henry lost.

With the overwhelming support of evangelicals, the assembly passed the Act for Establishing Religious

---

[40] James Madison, *To the Honorable the General Assembly of the Commonwealth of Virginia: A Memorial and Remonstrance.* Holograph manuscript, June 1785. Manuscript Division, Library of Congress.

Freedom. Unlike present-day Conservative Evangelicals, evangelicals in 1785 Virginia wanted no government involvement in religion, neither interference nor support. What explains the different attitudes of evangelicals across 225 years? Those in the Revolutionary Era were confident that if left free, they would succeed in spreading the Gospel. They believed their message was so powerful that it would prevail in the free marketplace of religion. Evangelicals today, especially the most Conservative, display a profound lack of confidence in their ability to prevail. Instead they blame the competition, claiming that "secularists" and "humanists" are dominating. Therefore, they seek closer ties with the state. In doing so, they tacitly admit that without government support they cannot compete.

The Contagion of Liberty and Disestablishment

As advocates of unfettered religious liberty retreated before the forces of religious establishment in Massachusetts and Connecticut, they fought a rearguard action. They found powerful weapons in the religious freedom safeguards of the United States Constitution and the First Amendment of the Bill of Rights. As the contagion of democracy and freedom spread in the first decades of the republic, the establishment clauses became more and more difficult to defend. They appeared more as Old World holdovers than New World freedom.

In 1789, James Madison took the initiative in drafting a Bill of Rights to the U.S. Constitution. As a leader in the fight for religious freedom in Virginia, he had opposed any grant of power to Congress over religion. At first, he had opposed a Bill of Rights, arguing that it was unnecessary because the states and the people retained all rights not explicitly granted to Congress; therefore, such rights as those of freedom of religion were protected. However, there had been such a clamor for a Bill of Rights to safeguard fundamental rights that he promised to seek amendments including one. In one draft, he sought to extend the kind of religious freedom enjoyed by Virginians to all the states. His proposed amendment read: "No state shall violate the equal rights of conscience, or the freedom of press, or the trial by jury in criminal cases."[41] His goal was to eliminate all state regulation of religion, including establishment laws and religious tests. Jealous of their states' rights over religion, most representatives rejected the measure.

Madison was not alone in working to eliminate state-supported and state-regulated religion. One of the leading fighters for religious liberty in Virginia was the Baptist minister John Leland. Leland was from Massachusetts, where his only formal education was that at elementary school, but he read widely and eventually became a Baptist minister. In 1776 he traveled to Virginia as a missionary and preached in Orange County, where he saw firsthand persecution of Baptists. He stayed in Virginia for fourteen years, and his friendship with Thomas Jefferson in the fight for religious freedom is one of the best examples of the kind of cooperation that took place between those from a primarily sacred perspective and those from a primarily secular viewpoint. After returning to Massachusetts in 1791, Leland took up the cause of disestablishment, first in Massachusetts, and then in Connecticut. Using arguments honed in Virginia, he sought for the New England states the same kind of outcome as he saw realized in Virginia: disestablishment combined with unfettered religious freedom.

---

[41] Cited in Jack Rakove, *Declaring Rights: A Brief History with Documents* (Boston: Bedford/St. Martin's, 1998) 173–74.

In 1791, he published in New London, Connecticut, a systematic and powerful treatise on religious liberty: *The Rights of Conscience Inalienable.* Like Jefferson, Leland declared that "religion is a matter between God and individuals, [and] religious opinions of men [are] not...the objects of civil government nor any ways under its control." He then argued that the Christian faith does not stand in need of any external support, including that of civil government, despite what proponents of establishment contended. "It has often been observed by the friends of religious establishment by human laws," he wrote, "that no state can long continue without it; that religion will perish, and nothing but infidelity and atheism prevail. Are these things facts?" He then proceeded to answer his question by turning to history:

> Did not the christian religion prevail during the three first centuries, in a more glorious manner than ever it has since, not only without the aid of law, but in opposition to all the laws of haughty monarchs? And did not religion receive a deadly wound by being fostered in the arms of civil power and regulated by law? These things are so. From that day to this we have but a few instances of religious liberty to judge by; for in almost all states civil rulers (by the instigation of covetous priests) have undertaken to steady the ark of religion by human laws; but yet we have a few of them without leaving our own land. The state of Rhode-Island has stood above 160 years without any religious establishment. The state of New-York never had any. New-Jersey claims the same. Pennsylvania has also stood from its first settlement until now upon a liberal foundation; and if agriculture, the mechanical arts and commerce, have not flourished in these states equal to any of the states I judge wrong.[42]

---

[42] Leland, *The Rights of Conscience Inalienable*, 9.

He then added that the wave of civil and religious freedom moving across the land was sweeping away establishment laws:

> It may further be observed, that all the states now in union, saving two or three in New-England, have no legal force used about religion, in directing its course or supporting its preachers. And moreover the federal government is forbidden by the constitution to make any laws establishing any kind of religion. If religion cannot stand, therefore, without the aid of law, it is likely to fall soon in our nation, except in Connecticut and Massachusetts.[43]

Leland concluded that the central argument advanced by advocates of establishment was demonstrably untrue. "To say that 'religion cannot stand without a state establishment' is not only contrary to fact (as has been proved already)," he reasoned, "but is a contradiction in phrase. Religion must have stood a time before any law could have been made about it; and if it did stand almost three hundred years without law it can still stand without it."[44]

Leland then turned to what he considered to be the "evils of establishment." Giving government a voice in religion is tantamount to allowing "[u]ninspired fallible men [to] make their own opinions tests of orthodoxy, and use their own systems, as Procrustes used his iron bedstead, to stretch and measure the consciences of all others by." Religious establishments are, in the second place, Leland maintained, "impolitic," especially in new countries, like the United States. He asked, "[W]hat encouragement can strangers have to migrate with their arts and wealth into a state where they cannot enjoy their religious sentiments

---

[43] Ibid.
[44] Ibid.

without exposing themselves to the law?" Not only will dissenters not go to a place where they do not enjoy religious freedom, they will flee from any place that ties their religious opinions to civil liberties. Leland asked further, "[H]ow often have kingdoms and states been greatly weakened by religious tests? In the time of the persecution in France not less than twenty thousand people fled for the enjoyment of religious liberty." Perhaps his most telling argument was that religious establishments frequently have the opposite effect from that intended. He explained,

> These establishments metamorphose the church into a creature, and religion into a principle of state; which has a natural tendency to make men conclude that bible religion is nothing but a trick of state. Hence it is that the greatest part of the well informed in literature are overrun with deism and infidelity: nor is it likely it will ever be any better while preaching is made a trade of emolument. And if there is no difference between bible religion and state religion I shall soon fall into infidelity.[45]

Leland's comments are a cautionary word to anyone wishing to create a Christian state. What is created is a state religion, and if history is any guide, that state religion will be opposed, not just by "secularists" but by those who embrace Bible religion, that is, religion according to their own interpretation of the Bible. Leland pointed out that state religions are man-made, which is evident when one compares two states purporting to embrace the same religious faith or creed. He noted, "In one kingdom a man is condemned for not believing a doctrine that he would be condemned for believing in another kingdom. Both of these

---

[45] Ibid., 11.

establishments cannot be right—but both of them can be, and surely are, wrong."[46]

The final evil that Leland listed centered on religious tests. Again, he argued that establishments and religious tests have unintended consequences, including that of keeping "from civil office the best of men." The honest man or woman will not subscribe to a test that calls for him or her to "take an oath to maintain what they conclude is error." In all states, he continued, the best of people differ over religious opinion and judgment, and if the state has a religious test, some of them whose "talents and virtue entitle them to fill the most important posts" cannot because "they differ from the established creed of the state." On the other hand, Leland warned, "villains make no scruple to take any oath."[47]

Lyman Beecher, pastor at Litchfield, Connecticut, was not persuaded by Leland's arguments. A staunch defender of the state's establishment (the Standing Order), he believed that disestablishment would usher in chaos with all sorts of dissenting groups competing for attention and souls. Yet, following the ratification of the U.S. Constitution, Republicans in the state had been relentless in pushing for disestablishment. Beecher returned to the oft-repeated argument that a religious establishment was the surest means for religious instruction, which, in turn, was essential for a virtuous citizenry. He thought religion too important to be left to the fate of voluntary contributions. People are subject to whim and distraction and may not sustain religious instruction at a level that would be guaranteed by the levy of taxes. But, alas, in 1818, with a growing number of Republicans demanding complete

---

[46] Ibid.
[47] Ibid., 11–12.

religious freedom, the Standing Order was overthrown and religious establishment in Connecticut was no more. In his *Autobiography,* Beecher lamented the day and called it "as dark a day as ever I saw." He added that attack on the established clergymen by people like Leland was vile and reprehensible. He wrote, "[T]he odium thrown upon the ministry was inconceivable. The injury done to the cause of Christ...was irreparable."[48]

Despite Beecher's opposition, dissenters succeeded in their fight for disestablishment in Connecticut. Article VII of the Constitution ratified in 1818 put religion on a voluntary basis with church members, only providing financing for maintaining the church. It read in part:

> It being the duty of all men to worship the Supreme Being, the great Creator and Preserver of the Universe, and their right to render that worship, in the mode most consistent with the dictates of their consciences; no person shall by law be compelled to join or support, nor be classed with, or associated to, any congregation, church, or religious association. But every person now belonging to such congregation, church, or religious association, shall remain a member thereof, until he shall have separated himself therefrom, in the manner hereinafter provided. And each and every society or denomination of christians in this state, shall have and enjoy the same and equal powers, rights, and privileges; and shall have power and authority to support and maintain the ministers or teachers of their respective denominations, and to build and repair houses for public worship, by a tax on the members of any such society only, to be laid by a major vote of the legal voters

---

[48] Barbara Cross, ed., *The Autobiography of Lyman Beecher,* 2 vols. (Cambridge MA: Harvard University Press, 1961) 1:252.

assembled at any society meeting, warned and held according to law, or in any other manner.[49]

The result of disestablishment was the creation of a competitive marketplace of religion, with all religious groups put on equal footing. Success in such an environment depended not on government favor but on the appeal of each group's message and the industry of its members and clergy in spreading that message. Under the new regime, religion thrived, leading Lyman Beecher to change his mind regarding disestablishment. In a reversal of opinion, he came to interpret the end of the Standing Order as *"the best thing that ever happened to the State of Connecticut."* Beecher's turnabout resulted from the revivals that broke out following disestablishment. In his words, "[T]he Lord began to pour out his Spirit." Ministers of all denominations worked together in organizing prayer meetings and preaching services to spread the Gospel. Beecher wrote that ministers had previously thought that their "children would scatter like partridges if the tax law was lost," but instead the effect was "just the reverse of the expectation."[50] Ministers became more industrious, and dissenters cooperated with former churchmen, resulting in a concerted attack on infidelity and a broad evangelical revival of religion.

Disestablishment took longer in Massachusetts, but in 1833 state-supported and regulated religion ended there. Similar to the constitutional provision in Connecticut, the prohibition against establishment in Massachusetts read: "[A]ll religious sects and denominations, demeaning

---

[49] The constitution for the state of Connecticut, 1818, is found at the Connecticut Secretary of State website: http://www.ct.gov/sots/cwp/view.asp?a=3188&q=392280 (accessed 8 August 2012).

[50] Cross, *Autobiography of Lyman Beecher*, 1:336–37.

themselves peaceably, and as good citizens of the commonwealth, shall be equally under the protection of the law; and no subordination of any one sect or denomination to another shall ever be established by law."[51] Now in all states, religion was placed on a voluntary basis, and no one was compelled to pay for the support of any religion he or she did not embrace. Disestablishment did not mean that the states no longer believed in the importance of religion in civil society. Most continued to think that religious instruction was the foundation of public virtue, but what had changed was the relation between church and state. All states now followed the federal model of prohibiting religious establishment and guaranteeing free exercise. However, several states continued to impose a religious test on officeholders, and some of those would continue in force well into the nineteenth century.

Some Conservatives, including Justice Clarence Thomas, argue that states continue to have the right to establish religion, just not a particular denomination. He insists that a state could establish Christianity as the state religion, but not the Methodist or the Baptist Church. South Carolina did just that in its constitution of 1778, declaring that the "Christian Protestant" religion was the established religion of the state. But even that broad construction failed to satisfy South Carolinians fired with the contagion of liberty. In the Constitution of 1808, all language regarding religious establishment was omitted, and there was no religious test. Officeholders were subject to a property-holding qualification only, and they swore to uphold the Constitution, not affirm a certain set of religious beliefs.

---

[51] The Constitution of Massachusetts, with 1833 alterations, is located at the Massachusetts General Court's website: http://www.malegislature.gov/laws/constitution (accessed August 20, 2013).

New states entering the union ratified constitutions with liberal clauses regarding religion. Vermont, the first state to join the original thirteen, stated the importance of religion to civil society and even voiced a preference for the Protestant faith. Nonetheless, religion was put on a voluntary basis, and free exercise was guaranteed. However, like their New England neighbors, there was a religious test: "I, _____, do believe in one God, the Creator and Governor of the Diverse, the rewarder of the good and punisher of the wicked. And I do acknowledge the scriptures of the old and new testament to be given by divine inspiration, and own and profess the protestant religion."[52] The next two states admitted, Kentucky and Tennessee, respectively, included clauses similar to that in the Virginia Statute for Religious Freedom. The Kentucky Constitution read in part: "no man can of right be compelled to attend, erect, or support any place of worship, or to maintain any ministry, against his consent; that no human authority can, in any case whatever, control or interfere with the rights of conscience; and that no preference shall ever be given by law to any religious societies or modes of worship."[53] The contagion of freedom meant that governments were to protect religion, not promote it. That would be left to individuals according to their consciences.

In 1776 Phillips Payson advocated state-supported religion because he thought it the best way to ensure religious instruction in society. He did not live to see the revival of religion that swept the nation in the first third of the nineteenth century, a revival so great it was called the

---

[52] The Vermont Constitution of 1786 is found in Thorpe, *The Federal and State Constitutions*, 3749–60.

[53] The Kentucky Constitution of 1792, ibid., 1264–76.

Great Awakening. Had he witnessed such an event, he would have no doubt been pleased with the spread of the Christian Gospel. Whether or not he would have been pleased with the particular Gospel being propagated is more problematic. Payson was a Calvinist, while the theology of the Great Awakening was Arminian. Differences within those professing the Christian faith mattered in the early republic, and they matter now, a point that Christian Right "historians" miss when they claim that the country was once a Christian nation. The question then and now is, *whose* Christianity? For both Thomas Jefferson and John Leland, the answer was the individual's, not the state's.

5

Constituting the Separation of Church and State in the New Republic

Christian Right "historians" are correct: the phrase "separation of church and state" does not appear in the U.S. Constitution or in any other founding document. Why, then, do many Americans regard separation of church and state as a sacred doctrine? Are Barton and other like-minded individuals correct in charging liberals and secularists with inventing the myth?

To James Madison, separation of church and state was no myth, but an expression of the broader principle of separation that he deemed essential for freedom. As he approached the Federal Convention in 1787, his central worry was that of strengthening the federal union without subverting individual liberty. He agreed with others like George Washington who saw a stronger, more powerful union as the guardian of American independence. But, at the same time, he feared a concentration of power, especially that of unchecked majority rule. Tyranny came in many guises; the colonists had come to regard monarchy as tyrannical, and Madison agreed. But he also believed that under a republic a majority could exercise a similar despotism.

To find the answer to his conundrum, Madison searched works of history and political theory, and in the end found his solution: separation. Madison's primary concerns were secular, involving ideas such as representation, taxation, rights, defense, and union. And his response was secular as well: preserve liberty by dividing power. Such an explanation runs counter to that of Religious Right "historians" who regard the Constitution as a Christian document aimed at creating a Christian state. In their telling, there is no place for the separation of church and state.

In his book, *Christianity and the Constitution: Faith of Our Founding Fathers,* John Eidsmoe accepts uncritically Thomas Jefferson's characterization of the delegates at the Federal Convention of 1787 as "an assembly of demigods." Eidsmoe goes further and opines that there never had been before and probably never will again be such an inspired assembly. Of course, he is far from alone in such unqualified praise for the men who drafted the U.S. Constitution. However, as a self-styled historian, he owes it to his readers to put Jefferson's phrase in context. Jefferson was in Paris at the time as the American Minister to France, and he wrote to John Adams, who was in London as Minster to England. Jefferson had learned the roster of delegates from James Madison, and he characterized the delegates as an "assembly of demigods." But, in that same letter to Adams, Jefferson also addressed their foibles as flawed human beings. Commenting on the first steps taken by the delegates, he commented, "I am sorry they began their deliberations by so abominable a precedent as that of tying up the tongues of their members. Nothing can justify this example but the innocence of their intentions, and ignorance of the value of public discussions. I have no doubt that all their other measures will be good and wise."[1]

---

[1] Thomas Jefferson to John Adams, 30 August 1787.

Jefferson was not the only founder to recognize the humanity of those who drafted the Constitution. On the last day of the Federal Convention, the delegates were seeking unanimous support for the draft, but three delegates, George Mason and Edmund Randolph of Virginia and Elbridge Gerry of Massachusetts, refused to sign the document. Mason proposed that in fairness to the people, in whose name the delegates had spoken, there should be a second convention that would take into account the concerns voiced by the people after they had had a chance to read and reflect on the document. He thought it wrong to present the draft to the states on a "take it or leave it" basis, as was the case because the delegates demanded from the ratifying conventions a vote that approved or disapproved without amendments. Franklin objected to a second convention, and in that objection reminded his colleagues that no human assembly, including the present one, is without flaws. In comments written for the occasion but read by James Wilson of Pennsylvania, Franklin wrote, "I doubt too whether any other Convention we can obtain may be able to make a better Constitution. For when you assemble a number of men to have the advantage of their joint wisdom, you inevitably assemble with those men, all their prejudices, their passions, their errors of opinion, their local interests, and their selfish views. From such an Assembly can a perfect production be expected?"[2] Franklin had great respect for the delegates and what they had accomplished, but he recognized that they were not "demigods," but self-interested and prejudiced mortals.

It was Jefferson himself who explained one of the undesired consequences of regarding the delegates as

---

[2] Max Farrand, ed., *The Records of the Federal Convention of 1787*, 3 vols. (New Haven CT: Yale University Press, 1911) 2:642.

demigods. In a letter to Samuel Kercheval dated 12 July 1816, Jefferson warned against viewing America's founding documents as timeless, changeless oracles good for all ages and circumstances.

> Some men look at constitutions with sanctimonious reverence, and deem them like the ark of the covenant, too sacred to be touched. They ascribe to the men of the preceding age a wisdom more than human, and suppose what they did to be beyond amendment...But I know also, that laws and institutions must go hand in hand with the progress of the human mind. As that becomes more developed, more enlightened, as new discoveries are made, new truths disclosed, and manners and opinions change with the change of circumstances, institutions must advance also, and keep pace with the times.[3]

Jefferson's sentiments about the need for a flexible constitution echoed those of fellow Virginian Edmund Randolph, who, as a member of the Committee of Detail, described the writing of the Constitution. He said that in writing the Constitution the committee inserted "essential principles only, lest the operations of government should be clogged by rendering those provisions permanent and unalterable, which ought to be accommodated to times and events."[4]

Many of the delegates at Philadelphia had participated in drafting state constitutions so they were experienced in the task at hand, a task that relied on clear thinking, keen negotiations, and practical compromises. Contrary to the revisionists' assertion that the founders created a miracle

---

[3] Thomas Jefferson to Samuel Kercheval, 12 July 1816, in Paul Leicester Ford, ed., *The Works of Thomas Jefferson*, 12 vols. (New York: G.P. Putnam's Sons, 1905) 12:11–12.

[4] Kurland and Lerner, eds., *The Founders' Constitution*, vol. 2, Preamble, doc. 7.

out of divine inspiration, John Adams regarded the state constitutions as secular instruments. Indeed, he thought what set apart American constitution-making from others throughout history is that reason rather than faith guided the framers. Writing in 1787 he declared, "The United States of America [represents] the first example of government erected on the simple principles of nature." The framers, he insisted, never had "interviews with the gods or were in any degree under the inspiration of Heaven." Rather, the state constitutions were "contrived merely by the use of reason and the senses." Thus, constitutions in the new republic were not the result of divine miracles; God did not hand down tablets inscribed with a frame of government. Rather than approaching the task of crafting constitutions as demigods awaiting oracular instruction, "Neither the people nor their conventions, committees, or subcommittees considered legislation in any other light than as ordinary arts and sciences, only more important." That is, the framers examined the needs of the day, considered the various constitutions that others had devised throughout history, and applied the principles they deemed to be best suited for their purposes. Adams credited the people of the Revolution for their enlightened constitutions: "The people were universally too enlightened to be imposed on by artifice.... Thirteen governments thus founded on the natural authority of the people alone, without a pretense of miracle or mystery, and which are destined to spread over the northern part of that whole quarter of the globe, are a great point gained in favour of the rights of mankind."[5] Having rejected monarchism and

---

[5] Charles Francis Adams, ed., *The Works of John Adams, Second President of the United States*, 10 vols. (Boston: Little, Brown and Company, 1856) 4:292–93.

divine right rule, Americans opted to live under rules devised by their own good judgment.

This chapter gets behind the myth that enshrouds the Federal Convention and examines the making of the Constitution. Specifically, it addresses the question of the separation of church as a constitutional principle. It also examines Eidsmoe's central argument in *Christianity and the Constitution* that the Constitution is a Calvinist document. Far from separating church and state, according to this interpretation, the delegates made sure that the Constitution conformed to Christian and biblical principles. To assess this assertion, we look first at the cluster of myths that have obscured our view of the Constitution and the context within which the Federal Convention takes place. Then we examine the principle of separation that Madison saw as the key to preserving liberty and explore how that principle applied to the place of religion in the new republic.

Myths of "the Founding Fathers" and the Making of the Constitution

Eidsmoe is hardly alone in taking a mythical view of the nation's founding. On 12 November 2010, Supreme Court Justices Antonin Scalia and Stephen Breyer debated the meaning and interpretation of the United States Constitution. While the two men often disagree on court decisions, they agreed that night on the origins of the Constitution. Both characterized the document as transcending history; Breyer called the document's emergence a "miracle," while Scalia called the writing of it "providential."[6] Both terms suggest that the document was

---

[6] See "Scalia, Breyer Spar Over Capital Punishment, Judicial Philosophy," posted on *Huffington Post* website:

the work of an extraordinary group of men whose deliberations were led by divine guidance. Such language is that found in Holy Scripture where God inspired men to write divine truth about God-led, history-changing moments such as Moses' delivering God's chosen people from the tyranny of the Egyptian pharaoh or the underdog David's slaying the giant Goliath.

In their debate, Scalia and Breyer gave voice to familiar myths surrounding the United States Constitution. First, both endorsed its miraculous birth, and while they did not use Jefferson's phrase, "assembly of demigods," to characterize the delegates, they viewed the authors as divinely inspired lawgivers. Second, Justice Scalia repeated his commitment to the doctrine of "original intent," that is, that the Constitution must be interpreted by examining the "original intent" of the delegates to the Federal Convention as well as those to the state ratifying conventions. In doing so, he supported the myth that the delegates' meaning is transparent and permanent. Those are but two of the many myths that Americans have created regarding the Constitution. Another is what historian Edmund Morgan calls the "fiction" of popular sovereignty, the notion that the people as a whole rule in the United States.[7] Other myths abound concerning the character of the delegates, their motivations and intentions, and the product of their deliberations. None is more enduring than that of the Constitution coming from the mind of a single genius. Early in the nation's history, James Madison was labeled the "Father of the Constitution," a label he denied with words but encouraged with deeds. Just as Americans prefer to see

---

http://www.huffingtonpost.com/2010/11/12/scalia-breyer-spar-capital-punishment_n_783081.html (accessed 8 August 2012). Betsy Blaney.

[7] Edmund Morgan, *Inventing the People: Rise of Popular Sovereignty in England and America* (New York: W.W. Norton & Co, 1988) 13–15.

Washington as winning the War of Independence and Jefferson writing the Declaration of Independence, they opt for a single author of the Constitution.

Ultraconservatives want to rewrite American history, literally. In 2012, Tennessee Tea Party activists proposed state laws that would force school districts to select textbooks guaranteeing that "no portrayal of minority experience in the history which actually occurred shall obscure the experience or contributions of the Founding Fathers." According to Hal Rounds, an attorney and a spokesman for the group, current texts included "an awful lot of made-up criticism about, for instance, the founders intruding on the Indians or having slaves or being hypocrites in one way or another." Thus, he and others who share his views wish to remove distortions in "the teaching of the history and character of the United States" by compelling teachers to impart to "students in Tennessee the truth regarding the history of our nation and the nature of its government."[8]

For Christian Right "historians," the "truth" of America's founding is self-evident, informed more by religious and political conviction than by historical investigation. But, to the founders themselves, the history of the founding was problematic to say the least. Secretary of the Continental Congress Charles Thomson understood firsthand the difficulty of writing an accurate account of the nation's founding when citizens wanted to believe in the fiction that their founding fathers were godlike beings. His position gave him a perfect vantage point for writing a

---

[8] Quoted in "Tea Party Groups in Tennessee Demand Textbooks Overlook U.S. Founder's Slave-Owning History," posted on *Huffington Post* website: http://www.huffingtonpost.com/2012/01/23/tea-party-tennessee-textbooks-slavery_n_1224157.html (accessed 8 August 2012). Trymaine Lee.

history of the men and events at the nation's beginning, but he forewent the writing of a history of the American Revolution because he feared that an account based on his notes, while factual, would expose the baser side of men being eulogized at the war's end. He had written a 1,000-word account of the revolution and was urged by friends to finish the book, but he then decided to burn his manuscript along with the notes and documents that supported it. He explained, "I could not tell the truth without giving great offense" because his writing was filled with the "intrigues and severe altercations or quarrels in the Congress." Rather, he mused, "Let the world admire our patriots and heroes." He knew that mythic accounts of the Revolution were already fixed in the minds of Americans, and if he published his version, it would "contradict all the histories of the great events of the Revolution." He justified his book-burning by declaring that the nation would be better served by "ignorance and misrepresentation" than accurate history because the "boasted 'talents and virtues' of the founding fathers would 'command imitation' and thus 'serve the cause of patriotism and of our country.'"[9]

While the founders warned against mythologizing the creation of the republic and its creators, subsequent generations have continued to spin myths that fit their own political views. Efforts to politicize history are not, of course, new. Indeed, the very term "the Founding Fathers" was invented by a politician seeking partisan advantage. The first instance of its usage in the long-running *New York Times* (1851–present) was in the 6 July 1920 issue, and that initial reference illustrates much of what the phrase has come to signify. It appeared in a quote from a speech

---

[9] Boyd Schlenther, *Charles Thomson, A Patriot's Pursuit* (Newark, DEL: University of Delaware Press, 1990) 204.

delivered by Warren G. Harding, who in mid-June had been nominated as the Republican Party's Presidential candidate. On 5 July he addressed a hometown crowd in Marion, Ohio. Making his remarks a day after Independence Day celebrations, Harding struck a patriotic theme. From the semicircular veranda of his "modest green-painted house," he addressed a crowd of about 3,000, nearly all of whom were his friends and neighbors from Marion. The name of the street on which his house was located was Mount Vernon Avenue, an appellation that conjured images of the founding fathers, whose memory Harding evoked in his speech. Noting that the people had been observing "the anniversary of the Republic's independence," Harding called for a return to the nation's founding: "Let us pledge ourselves anew one and all that this heritage handed to us through the heroism and sacrifices of the founding fathers shall be here sacred, unabridged and undimmed." Harding's reference to "the founding fathers" was not his last. In another speech he again made a connection between his ideas of government and politics and those of the founders. "It was the interest of the founding fathers," he said, "to give to this republic a dependable and enduring popular Government, representative in form, and it was designed to make political parties not only the preserving sponsors but also the effective agencies through which hopes and aspirations and convictions and conscience may be translated into public performance."[10] His reference to popular government was part of his campaign pledge to "return" government to the hands of "normal" people rather than the "supermen," as he characterized the Democrats under

---

[10] "Neighbors Turnout to Greet Harding...", *New York Times*, 6 July 1920.

Woodrow Wilson's administration. And, his reference to political parties was part of his vow to rise above petty partisanship and offer sound government to the people.

Harding's invocation of the founders reminds us that Americans have two sets of founders: those that created America, and those that Americans create. The first are the many historical figures who, in the last quarter of the eighteenth century, declared and fought for independence and created a new republic. The second are those few mythological figures, designated "the founding fathers," that are conjured in the minds of patriots and partisans, like Harding, to validate a particular set of values or interests.

While America's mythmakers depict the nation's founding as a miraculous moment brought about by the efforts of a few demigods, the founders themselves viewed it as a struggle occurring over a long period of time and the work of an entire generation. The founders could not agree on exactly when the American Revolution began. John Adams thought it started after the French and Indian War. He wrote, "The Revolution was effected before the war commenced. The Revolution was in the minds and hearts of the people. This radical change in the principles, opinions, sentiments, and affections of the people was the real American Revolution." Benjamin Rush disagreed. Writing in 1787 on the eve of the Federal Convention in Philadelphia, he said, "[T]here is nothing more common than to confound the terms of the American Revolution with those of the late American War. The war is over, but this is far from being the case with the American Revolution. On the contrary, nothing but the first act of the great drama is closed."[11] So for those who saw their world

---

[11] Colleen A. Sheehan, *Friends of the Constitution: Writings of the "Other" Federalists, 1787–1788,* ed. Colleen A. Sheehan and Gary L.

turned upside down, the beginning was unclear. What is clearer is that the Revolution was a process, a long process filled with contingency. Those who contributed to it did not work in concert from a single blueprint toward an agreed-upon goal. Rather, individuals and groups followed their own experiences and beliefs and took certain actions whose outcomes were uncertain. For instance, in 1793, accustomed to buying and selling tea under their own control, they reacted to the Tea Act, under which only designated merchants could sell the tea and under which the three-pence duty would be collected by a beefed-up force of customs agents. When the colonists protested by destroying private property (the tea belonged to the East India Company), Parliament imposed severe strictures on Massachusetts's government and commerce. In response to that crackdown, colonists from all over British North America began to organize for concerted protest. Thousands of people were involved.

But Americans prefer the story of a few giants—demigods—working a miracle to a more complicated tale involving thousands of soldiers, statesmen, merchants, ministers, and ordinary citizens who fought for independence and established a new republic.

Like the Declaration of Independence the U.S. Constitution has taken on the stature of Holy Writ, and every utterance of the delegates who drafted it as well as those who ratified it has been parsed in the search for "original intent." James Madison, unquestionably the leading architect at the Federal Convention and one of most

McDowell (Indianapolis: Liberty Fund, 1998), 1. Benjamin Rush "Address to the People of the United States," in *The Works of John Adams*, 10.282. (Indianapolis: Liberty Fund, 1998, 1. http://oll.libertyfund.org/title/2069/156135/2769916 (accessed 10 March 2013).

eloquent spokesmen for ratification, especially in his essays contributed to *The Federalist Papers*, cautioned against interpreting the Constitution by seeking the "original intent" of those who framed and ratified it. He knew firsthand of the many opinions expressed at Philadelphia and Williamsburg (site of Virginia's Ratifying Convention) and the heated debates that at times seemed to threaten the document's passage and ratification. He knew that there was no single "intent," as subsequent debates over the Constitution illustrated. He warned, "As a guide in expounding and applying the provisions of the Constitution, the debates and incidental decisions of the Convention can have no authoritative character." He thought that only a perspective far removed in time from the heated debates of 1787 and 1788 could produce a cooler judgment of what the Constitution meant. In his mind, that time should be at least "till the Constitution should be well settled by practice, and till a knowledge of the controversial part of the proceedings of its framers could be turned to no improper account...."[12]

Those who regard the U.S. Constitution as secular scripture miraculously conceived in Philadelphia during summer 1787 tend to ignore contingency or disregard it in the proceedings. In fact, while words like "miracle" and "scripture" figure large in our myth of the republic's beginnings, the delegates were men who believed that they and they alone would have to find a way to form a "more perfect Union." Unlike the Puritan fathers 150 years before them, who believed that God intervened directly in history and directed human events, the delegates in 1787 had a different view. They thought that people were to use their God-given reason to imagine and build a better world, and

---

[12] Hunt, ed., *The Writings of James Madison*, 9:71–72.

when that was done, they were willing to pronounce it a result of God's Providence. Instead of a miracle, the Constitution was hammered out by "bargain & compromise," according to New Hampshire delegate Nicholas Gilman.[13]

The delegates at Philadelphia knew that they had not produced a perfect instrument. No one worked harder for ratification of the Constitution than Alexander Hamilton, and yet he was aware that the draft was flawed. Opponents, he wrote in *Federalist 85*, asked, "Why...should we adopt an imperfect thing? Why not amend it and make it perfect before it is irrevocably established?" Hamilton responded, "[T]hough it may not be perfect in every part, [it] is, upon the whole, a good one; [it] is the best that the present views and circumstances of the country will permit; and [it] is such an one [sic] as promises every species of security which a reasonable people can desire." He acknowledged that the Constitution was based on concessions and compromise, a necessity in a country of diverse interests. Hamilton contended that "the result of the deliberations of all collective bodies must necessarily be a compound, as well of the errors and prejudices, as of the good sense and wisdom, of the individuals of whom they are composed." But, he added, the task at Philadelphia was even more challenging: "The compacts which are to embrace thirteen distinct States in a common bond of amity and union, must as necessarily be a compromise of as many dissimilar interests and inclinations. How can perfection spring from such materials?"[14] So to the delegates at the ratifying

---

[13] Nicholas Gilman to Joseph Gilman, dated 18 September 1787, in Farrand, *Records of the Federal Convention*, 3:82. .

[14] See Alexander Hamilton, *Federalist 85*. In the Library of Congress Online Edition of *The Federalist Papers*. See Thomas.loc.gov/histdox/fedpapers.html. Accessed August 20, 2013.

conventions, he urged, consider the draft not as a divinely inspired, perfect instrument that satisfies each partial or partisan perspective, but as a solid and workable, though imperfect, document that assumes an impartial or national view.

Religion and the Quest for a "More Perfect Union"

For John Eidsmoe, the Federal Convention of 1787 was about creating a Christian state. To make his case, he presents the delegates as godly Christians, and then he interprets their draft of the Constitution as a document that conforms to Calvinist and biblical principles. Eidsmoe claims in *Christianity and the Constitution* that the delegates based the Constitution on Calvinism, and the first source he cites is a work that he calls a source "that stands out above all others." Rather than a primary source taken from the founding era, it is a book by E.W. Smith, a nineteenth-century Presbyterian theologian. Smith's interpretation of America's founding came not from examining the writings of the founders, but from his theological conviction. Thus, in his book, *The Creed of Presbyterians*, E.W. Smith asks of American colonists, "Where learned they those immortal principles of the rights of man, of human liberty, equality and self-government, on which they based their Republic, and which form today the distinctive glory of our American civilization? In the school of Calvin they learned them. There the modern world learned them. So history teaches." For Eidsmoe, that assertion is proof enough. He does add similar assertions, but his case does not rest upon a thorough examination of the delegates' writings interpreted within historical context. When one does so, it is clear that religion was not the primary purpose or inspiration in writing the Constitution.

It can be argued that Madison took the lead at the Federal Convention because he was the best prepared. He arrived on 14 May with others in the Virginia delegation, fully prepared with a stinging indictment of the Articles of Confederation and a framework for a new constitution. In doing so, Madison set the terms of debate for the delegates at Philadelphia. For George Washington, a stronger union was what the country needed. As commander of the Continental Army during the War of Independence, Washington had witnessed firsthand the weakness of a government based on the voluntary contributions of the individual states. First, the Second Continental Congress, and then, Congress under the Articles of Confederation possessed no independent taxing authority and were compelled to ask the states for funds for prosecuting the war. Fearful of consolidated power as they had lived under as British subjects, newly independent Americans were unwilling to vest taxing authority with a distant body. Thus, the power of the purse resided in the states. As a result, the funds flowing to the Continental Army were sometimes slow, sometimes short, and always frustrating to Washington. Indeed, he blamed the prolongation of the war, and as a result, the mounting casualties, on the unwillingness or inability of local governments to pay the bills of freedom. On 8 June 1783, just two years after the defeat of the British at Yorktown, Washington sent a message to all the governors, urging them to put aside state and local jealousies in order to strengthen the Union. He wrote:

> [I]t is indispensable to the happiness of the individual states, that there should be lodged somewhere, a supreme power to regulate and govern the general concerns of the...republic, without which the Union cannot be of long duration. That there must' be a faithful and pointed

compliance on the part of every state, with the...proposals and demands of Congress, or the most fatal consequences will ensue; that whatever measures have a tendency to dissolve the Union, or contribute to violate or lessen the sovereign authority, ought to be considered as hostile to the liberty and independency of America, and the authors of them treated accordingly....[W]ithout an entire conformity to the spirit of the Union, we cannot exist as an independent power.[15]

Fellow Virginian, James Madison, was an early advocate for a convention to revise the Articles of Confederation, and, like Washington, Madison was concerned about union, not religion. He, along with other delegates such as George Washington, James Wilson, Alexander Hamilton, and Benjamin Franklin, believed that the young republic's future depended on the delegates not only amending the articles but putting in place a new form of government that would strengthen the bonds of union.

The country was beset with threats from abroad and instability at home. While Britain had recognized American independence in 1783, Parliament had refused to negotiate a commercial treaty with the U.S. Moreover, the British locked Americans out of the lucrative West Indies trade. Spain held title to the huge Louisiana Territory, and fearing the Americans as commercial rivals, closed the Mississippi River to American navigation. And beginning in 1784, the "petty powers" (Jefferson's phrase) of Africa's Barbary Coast captured American merchant vessels and closed the Mediterranean to U.S. shipping. At home, the country's fiscal state was dire with continental notes issued during the Revolutionary War, having depreciated to only one-

---

[15] John FitzPatrick, ed., *The Writings of George Washington from the Original Manuscript Sources, 1745–1790* (Wash DC: Govt Printing Office, 1931–44), 26:488–89

tenth their face value. As returning soldiers in western Massachusetts sought to resume their lives, they faced foreclosure on their farms because they could not pay their taxes in the post-war recession with their severely depreciated currency. Led by veteran Daniel Shays, they organized an armed tax revolt against what they deemed to be unfair taxation from Boston, thus initiating civil war in Massachusetts. Facing such problems, Madison and others sought a remedy through reconstituting the government altogether.

Madison's preparation for strengthening the union through a more powerful central government belies Eidsmoe's claim that John Calvin was the primary inspiration of the Constitution. For more than three years before the Federal Convention finally convened in Philadelphia in 1787, Madison immersed himself in works of history, not of theology. To understand how the Constitution came into being, one must begin with the thoughts and concerns of its leading architect months and even years before the Federal Convention of 1787. On 16 March 1784, James Madison wrote his friend Thomas Jefferson requesting history books on confederacies. It is unclear if Madison thought that Jefferson might have such works in his private library or if Madison was anticipating Jefferson's 7 May appointment as minister plenipotentiary to Paris. At any rate, Madison wanted to begin a systematic study of historical confederacies in order to understand how they worked and why they failed. On 14 November, having arrived in France in August, Jefferson informed Madison that he had purchased a "few books" for him and would soon ship them. Over the next several months, Madison added to his request and exhibited impatience when new books were slow in arriving. On 20 August 1785, he informed Jefferson, "I have not yet received any of the books" from his latest request. A month later, before Jefferson had received the note, Jefferson informed his young friend that he had sent two trunks filled with "your books." On 12 May 1786, still a year before the Convention opened, Madison acknowledged the receipt of Jefferson's latest shipment of books and then asked Jefferson to send him the *Encyclopedie*. Published in thirty-five volumes over the period spanning 1751 to 1772, this massive work represented the thought of the French Enlightenment, and the aim of its editor, Denis Diderot, was revolutionary: "to change the way people think." Its contributors included such Enlightenment luminaries as Diderot, d'Alembert, Voltaire, Rousseau, and Montesquieu. Organized under three branches of human knowledge—Memory/History, Reason/Philosophy, and Imagination/Poetry—the *Encyclopedie* attacked traditional authority and superstition, including that which passed as religious teachings in Holy Scripture. In ordering the *Encyclopedie*, Madison expanded his reading from a historical inquiry into confederations to the latest thinking about natural rights and political theory.[16]

A further indication of what Madison read and how he prepared for the Federal Convention is found in the list of books that he recommended the Continental Congress purchase for its members' use. In 1783, he, along with Thomas Mifflin of Pennsylvania and Hugh Williamson of North Carolina, was charged with the task of identifying the books. Although the lack of funds ultimately prevented the purchase of the books, the list itself is instructive in understanding what works Madison deemed important for

---

[16] Hunt, ed., *The Writings of James Madison*, vol. 2. Discussion of books requested and ordered found in Madison's letters to Thomas Jefferson beginning 24 March 1784 through 12 May 1786.

lawmakers. The first category bore the heading, "Law of Nature and Nations," and included such works as Cudworth's *Intellectual System*, Cumberland's *Law of Nature*, Wolfius's *Law of Nature*, Hutchinson's *Moral Philosophy*, Beller's *Delineation of Universal Law*, Ferguson's analysis of *Mor: Philosophy*, Rutherforth's *Institutes of Natural Law*, Grotius's *Law of Nature and Nations*, Puffendorf's *Law of Nature and Nations* (with notes by Barbeyrac), Puffendorf's *de officio hominis et civis*, Vattell's *Law of Nature and Nations* and *Questions in Natural Law*, and Burlamaque's *Law of Nature and Nations*. Other categories include histories from France, England, Russia, Spain, Rome, and Greece. Books in foreign languages abound. In short, the compilation is just what one would expect from an educated, eighteenth-century, enlightened intellectual. What is missing from the long list of titles, however, is any work by Calvin. If Eidsmoe's claim is correct, one would expect to see, at minimum, Calvin's *Institutes of the Christian Religion*. That it is not speaks to the secular, not sacred, task that Madison and his colleagues undertook.[17]

For Madison, who took the lead in drafting a blueprint for the delegates to follow at the convention, the challenge was how to increase the power of the central government without diminishing individual rights. What he found daunting was how to do that in a country as vast as the U.S. Republics throughout history had succeeded only in small territories, like the city-states of Italy. Large-scale republics like that of Rome had failed. After reading works of the Scottish Enlightenment thinker David Hume, Madison realized that a far-flung country could work to protect freedom. He recognized that the U.S., as all countries were,

---

[17] Library of Congress, *Journals of the Continental Congress, 1774–1789*, 34 vols. (Washington, D.C.: Library of Congress, 1904–1937) 24:83–92.

was deeply divided by factions. Americans were divided by economic interests, with some pursuing agriculture, others commerce, and still others manufacturing. They were also divided by cultural, especially religious, differences, with Protestants fractured into numerous competing sects. If advocates of a particular interest could organize themselves into a powerful single group, they could possibly impose their will on the entire country. When Madison realized that building a powerful interest group would be much more difficult in a large territory where the population was spread out than within a small area such as that of a state, he grew confident that an American republic could in fact work.

"Separation of Church and State": Constitutional Principle of Religious Freedom

David Ramsay of South Carolina, who wrote one of the earliest histories of the American Revolution, viewed the separation of church and state as one of the most revolutionary results of the War of Independence. He proclaimed that "all religious establishments were abolished," a statement that was not quite accurate at the time because Connecticut and Massachusetts retained establishments until 1818 and 1833, respectively. He noted that some states "retained a constitutional distinction between Christians and others, with respect to eligibility to office, but the idea of supporting one denomination at the expence of others…was universally reprobated." Thus as delegates traveled to Philadelphia for the Federal Convention of 1787 to amend the Articles of Confederation, the place of religion had been settled by the states, and, as Ramsay put it, "the alliance between church and state was completely broken," and in the future "each was left to support itself, independent of the other."[18]

Much had changed between 1776 and 1787. Indeed, historian Gordon Wood has argued that 1776 and 1787 were separate revolutionary moments. 1776 was a republican revolution that saw Patriots coming together to overthrow an oppressive imperial ruler, and the rallying cries were equality and virtue in service of the public good. People were considered to have inalienable natural rights, and they were deemed to be sovereign rulers who entrusted the protection of their rights to elected representatives, whom they held strictly accountable. These ideas animated the Declaration of Independence and found expression in the state constitutions. 1787, on the other hand, was a federalist revolution that shifted power from the states to the central government. The reasons for this revolution suggest that something had gone awry with republicanism. A growing number of influential Americans, including some of the most revered founders, namely James Madison, George Washington, Benjamin Franklin, and Alexander Hamilton, were alarmed at what they considered to be factional abuses of popular sovereignty. State legislatures were passing legislature that favored special interests rather than the public good. Liberal bankruptcy laws favored debtors over creditors; tax codes favored the poorer sorts over the richer sorts; and an expanding franchise favored the landless or small holders over large landholders.

When the delegates convened at Philadelphia in May 1787, they arrived more as salvage-workers than miracle workers. That is, their mission as authorized by Congress

---

[18] David Ramsay, *The History of the American Revolution (Selections)*, in Charles S. Hyneman, *American Political Writing During the Founding Era: 1760–1805*, 2 vols (Indianapolis: The Liberty Fund, 1983) 1:248–49..

was to recommend changes to the flawed Articles of Confederation. Five of the delegates had had a hand in crafting the articles, and now they considered how to correct their most glaring weaknesses. Moreover, the articles were based on principles many then and now regard as sacrosanct, including those of limited government and states' sovereignty. But, the country under the articles was beset by foreign threats, domestic insurrection, and fiscal collapse. While the Parliament had recognized U.S. independence in the Peace of Paris (1783), it refused to enter into a commercial treaty with the new republic. In fact, Britain closed its West Indian ports to American ships. In addition, Spain refused to grant Americans access to the Mississippi River and the Port of New Orleans. Further impeding trade in the West, Native Americans, backed by a continued British military presence along the frontier, thwarted westward expansion. And the "petty" Barbary States along North Africa captured a few U.S. trading ships and effectively closed the Mediterranean to American shipping. As if all these foreign threats were not enough, the United States faced problems at home. The country was in effect bankrupt. Without independent taxing authority, Congress could not generate sufficient revenue for a stable currency. Consequently, the continental notes issued during the War of Independence to pay soldiers and suppliers plummeted in value. Some of those soldiers lost their property because they could not pay their mortgages. In Massachusetts, Daniel Shays sought justice through a rebellion aimed at the government at Boston, plunging that state into civil war and raising the prospects of even wider domestic disorder.

Thus, the delegates focused primarily on pressing and immediate challenges facing the republic at the time, not those of future circumstances that they could not possibly foresee. To be sure, they were mindful of the future and sought to draft a frame of government on broad principles that future generations could adapt to their own circumstances. And they worried that future generations might not be as "liberal" and "enlightened" as they. But their primary focus was on their present, not that of future Americans.

The Preamble to the Constitution sets forth the purposes of government as conceived by the delegates, and each of the six purposes was aimed at problems confronting the nation in 1787. While Americans of subsequent generations have thought of the founders as writing a constitution that would last for centuries, the delegates were primarily concerned about the immediate concerns facing them. A look at the Preamble underscores the point: To "form a more perfect Union" was an acknowledgment that the existing union under the articles was imperfect. To "establish Justice" meant equal treatment of all white people and all states under the law, a touchy subject given the varying sizes and interests of the states, especially the sectional split over slaveholding. To "insure domestic Tranquility" was directed toward preventing such civil disturbances as Shays' Rebellion. To "provide for the common defence" recognized that the United States was beset on all sides by enemies threatening the country's interests and people, including the British, Native Americans, Spain, and Barbary Pirates. To "promote the general Welfare" was an ambiguous phrase but included at least the provision of infrastructure and education. And to "secure the Blessings of Liberty to ourselves and our Posterity" provided the rationale for a central government with sufficient power to safeguard freedom for Americans at home and abroad.

The challenges that religion presented the delegates were far greater than those faced by state constitutional conventions. The religious landscape of the United States was different from that of any single state and certainly different from that of the early colonial settlements. First, there was great and growing diversity. The eighteenth century had witnessed the arrival of many new dissenting groups, especially in Pennsylvania. The Great Awakening had sparked divisions and separations that resulted in new groups of Baptists and Methodists and Presbyterians. And during the Revolutionary era, new churches, inspired in part by the "contagion of liberty," emerged, including the Unitarian and Universalist Churches. Second, the fastest-growing churches were evangelical congregations, especially the Baptists and Methodists. With their aggressive preaching and wide-ranging itinerancies, they reached far beyond settled communities in the East and provided the Gospel to people along the frontier, and by the mid-1800s, these two groups were the largest denominations both in the number of members and the number of churches. Third, religious differences mattered to all these Protestant groups. They held much in common, such as the belief that Scripture alone was sufficient for salvation, that each person was his or her own priest and stood alone before God, and that salvation was by grace through faith alone, not by works. But they also differed on matters of theology, biblical interpretation, and polity, matters that to outsiders might appear to be minor but to those inside a particular confession were major indeed. And, fourth, there was a growing insistence among dissenters for full religious freedom, not just whatever a state was willing to tolerate, but liberty of conscience that extended public as well as private worship and instruction.

The religious profile of the delegates at Philadelphia bears scrutiny. Christian Right "historians" usually categorize the delegates by their church membership and then amass every quotation on religion uttered by each delegate in order to demonstrate that they were Christians. From this they wish to leave the impression that the delegates were devout and devoted Christians who were fired by Christian principles to create a Christian Constitution. Such analysis does not link belief to behavior. First, religious affiliation or stated beliefs do not necessarily explain behavior. Christian politicians and Christian businessmen and Christian ballplayers frequently do many un-Christian things. Second, people assume many different roles and often compartmentalize those various roles so that a devout elder in a church on Sunday is also a hard-driving merchant or broker on Monday, and sometimes the beliefs and rules followed on the Sabbath have little to do with the realities faced in the counting house or stock exchange. Christian teachings of loving one's neighbor might prompt acts of charity in the same person who does all he or she can to bury the competition in markets where the fight for capital and markets is keen.

There are several things that can be said about the delegates' beliefs with a high degree of certainty. First, they were overwhelmingly Protestant Christians in their religious affiliations. Only one of the signers of the Constitution was a Roman Catholic, Charles Carroll of Carrollton, Maryland. And only Benjamin Franklin could be labeled deist. Most of the others were members of the dominant Protestant churches of the period, primarily Anglican or Episcopal, Congregational, and Presbyterian. Second, they all believed that God created the universe and that God's Providence directed human affairs. Franklin, in particular, and deists in general, believed in God as Creator and Superintendent of Affairs. That said, the delegates also believed that they were active agents in history and did not wait passively for some divine sign before they acted. Moreover, their comments on acts of Providence usually followed rather than preceded events. George Washington, among others, acknowledged Providence in leading Americans to victory in the War of Independence, but he believed that wars were won by well-supplied, well-trained, and well-lead armies. Third, the delegates expressed their belief in a higher law, God's law. It is true that in discussing that law they often emphasized the God of Nature who was the author of natural rights, rather than the God of the Old Testament that demanded obedience in exchange for protection. Fourth, the delegates emphasized morality over theology in their public statements of religion, especially on the utility of religion in public life. They regarded theological views largely as private matters that sometimes surfaced in public dispute, but they thought that moral teachings influenced the way men and women behaved. Contrary to Barton and Eidsmoe, the delegates rarely ever mentioned Calvinism or Calvinist teachings, but they did talk about honesty and integrity. And, fifth, the delegates believed in religious liberty, and most believed that the individual, not the state, should direct religious affairs.

The founders were not, however, in total agreement on religion. First, the place and importance of Jesus were sometimes contentious. Thomas Jefferson and John Adams, along with Benjamin Franklin, denied the divinity of Jesus, while at the same time accepting his moral teachings as sublime. Most other delegates seldom referred to Jesus in their public statements. Second, personal statements on religion said little about how devoted individual delegates were in their observance of public worship. According to

George Washington's diary, there were years when entries about the Sabbath contained more accounts of hunting than of attending divine services. Third, some of the founders were freethinkers, meaning they interpreted the Bible according to their own lights and not according to what a denomination might deem orthodox. None went as far as Jefferson, who proclaimed himself to be a church of one, but, nonetheless, these were not men who bowed passively to clerical pronouncements.

To Madison and his fellow delegates, religion represented a possible impediment to creating a more perfect union. Many of them had participated in state constitutional conventions and knew firsthand how divisive religious questions could become. Moreover, they were aware that, given the religious diversity in the country, any religious settlement would likely be controversial, and, certainly, any religious establishment, no matter how broadly conceived, would be unacceptable. Therefore, for the most part the delegates ignored religion at the Federal Convention.

Given their priorities and the potential divisiveness of sectarianism, the delegates seldom mentioned religion at the convention and at the state ratifying conventions. A keyword search of the proceedings at the Federal Convention at Philadelphia and the state ratifying conventions reveals, for instance, that religion and religious faith were rarely discussed. At Philadelphia, the name of Christ is not recorded in any of the surviving notes taken by James Madison, Robert Yates, Alexander Hamilton, and others, and it appears just four times in the debates of the state conventions. The name of Jesus does not appear in the federal notes, and but twice in the states' records. The Bible is mentioned twice and six times, respectively. God's name is invoked twelve times at Philadelphia and thirty-six times in the ratifying conventions, but not always in a reverent way. Some usages were rather profane, such as "Good God, Sir..." and "God knows how many more times...." And, despite Eidsmoe's insistence that Calvinism predominated at the convention, there is no mention at all of Calvin, Calvinism, or Calvin's *Institutes of the Christian Religion*. And contrary to Sarah Palin's repeated insistence that the founders were guided by the Ten Commandments, they make no mention of them in their deliberations.

Religion arose as an issue just twice at the Federal Convention. The first time occurred on Thursday, 28 June, after weeks of debate on the thorny question of representation. Delegates had divided over whether each state should have the same number of votes in Congress or if votes should be apportioned by population. Benjamin Franklin, noting the "small progress" made during the past five weeks, suggested that the delegates turn to "that kind providence [to which] we owe this happy opportunity of consulting in peace on the means of establishing our future national felicity." He suggested that the delegates lift their eyes from their petty jealousies and local interests that divided them to their Creator that united them. "I have lived, Sir, a long time," he remarked, "and the longer I live, the more convincing proofs I see of this truth—that God governs in the affairs of men." He compared the partisan wrangling at the convention to the confusion attending the building of the Tower of Babel. Without the help of God, he declared, "We shall be divided by our little partial local interests; our projects will be confounded, and we ourselves shall become a reproach and bye word down to future ages. And what is worse, mankind may hereafter from this unfortunate instance, despair of establishing Governments by Human Wisdom and leave it to chance, war, and conquest."[19] He proposed that the delegates hire local clergymen to open future sessions with prayer. Christian Right "historian" William Federer is but one of several who claim that Franklin's speech turned the tide of the convention. Federer wrote, "The Constitutional Convention was in a deadlock over how large and small states could be represented equally. Some delegates gave up and left. Then, on 28 June 1787, 81-year-old Benjamin Franklin spoke and shortly after, the U.S. Constitution became a reality."[20] His conclusion represents the logical fallacy of *post hoc ergo propter hoc* (after this, therefore, because of this). It is a fallacy of causation that claims that the presence of something is responsible for what follows. No doubt some delegates were moved by Franklin's remarks; others were not. Roger Sherman and others supported the resolution and argued that it "would at least be as likely to do good as ill." Alexander Hamilton and others pointed out that if the matter had come up at the beginning of the convention, they would probably view it in a different light. But, suggesting that the delegates should, in the midst of a critical debate, hire a chaplain and turn to God for answers, might "bring on it some disagreeable animadversions" and "lead the public to believe that the embarrassments and dissentions within the convention, had suggested this measure."[21] In other words, it would hardly inspire confidence in the people's trust in their delegates to solve knotty problems. Writing years later, James Madison recalled that, because of respect for Franklin, the measure

---

[19] Farrand, *Records of the Federal Convention*, 1:450–52.

[20] See William Federer, "Do We Imagine We No Longer Need God's Assistance?", posted on 28 June 2012, http://www.americanclarion.com/9447/2012/06/28/imagine-longer-gods-assistance/ (accessed August 20, 2013).

[21] Farrand, *Records of the Federal Convention*, 1:452.

was referred to a committee, where it died. Franklin offered a terse comment on the outcome of his motion: "The Convention, except three or four persons, thought Prayers unnecessary."[22]

The second instance in which religion became an issue was in regard to the question of religious tests for federal officeholders. On 20 August, the Committee of Detail presented several propositions for consideration, including the following: "No religious test or qualification shall ever be annexed to any oath of office under the authority of the U.S." Ten days later, with little discussion, the measure passed unanimously. While some states retained religious tests in their constitution, there would be none imposed by Congress.

When the draft constitution was debated in the state ratifying conventions, three objections arose concerning religion. First, some were appalled at the lack of any acknowledgment of God or God's Providence in creating the Constitution. Typical reaction was that of one letter-writer to a Boston newspaper, dated 10 January 1788. The writer warned that because God was left out of the Constitution, Americans would suffer the fate foretold in Samuel: "because thou hast rejected the word of the Lord, he hath also rejected you." Another Massachusetts writer commented that "public inattention" to religion was a major flaw of the draft constitution, and he, too, predicted disaster. "It is more difficult to build an elegant house without tools to work with," the writer argued, "than it is to establish a durable government without the publick protection of religion." In the 18 February 1888 *American Mercury*, a commentator writing as Elihu responded to

---

[22] Ibid.

those who objected "that God has no seat allowed" in the proposed constitutional government. He wrote,

> A low mind may imagine that God, like a foolish old man, will think himself slighted and dishonored if he is not complimented with a seat or a prologue of recognition in the Constitution, but those great philosophers who formed tile Constitution had a higher idea of the perfection of that INFINITE MIND which governs all worlds than to suppose they could add to his honor or glory, or that He would be pleased with such low familiarity or vulgar flattery.

He lauded the delegates for drafting a constitution in plain language based on common sense, avoiding "all appearance of craft, declining to dazzle even the superstitious by a hint about grace or ghostly knowledge." Rather than trying to present themselves as miracle-workers, the delegates "come to us in the plain language of common sense and propose to our understanding a system of government as the invention of mere human wisdom; no deity comes down to dictate it, nor even a God appears in a dream to propose any part of it." Yet, he concluded, "there are not wanting FANATICS who would crown it with the periwig of an old monk and wrap it up in a black cloak—whilst political quackery is contending to secure it with fetters and decorate it with a leather apron!"[23] Elihu's sentiments apply as well to present-day attempts to make the Constitution a miraculous, divinely inspired work of demigods.

A second objection was the absence of a religious test. Amos Singletary, a delegate to the Massachusetts convention, thought it absurd that the Constitution of a Christian nation should not mandate that all officeholders under it be Christians. And yet, he noted in disbelief, "by

---

[23] Located in Sheehan, *Friends of the Constitution*, 1998) 345.

the Constitution, a papist, or an infidel was as eligible as" a Christian.[24] Similarly, David Caldwell, a delegate to the North Carolina convention, feared that the open "invitation to Jews and pagans" meant that it is "most certain, that Papists may occupy that chair [i.e., the presidency], and Mahometans may take it."[25] Isaac Backus, speaking at the Massachusetts Ratifying Convention, provided a compelling argument against religious tests. He noted that according to Scripture and reason, religion is a matter between the individual and God, and is not an affair of the state. Turning to history, he noted that when the Roman emperor Constantine "adopted the profession of Christianity as an engine of state policy," Christians, although no longer persecuted, found the hand of government intruding on the Church. Backus contended, "[L]et the history of all nations be searched from that day to this, and it will appear that the imposing of *religious tests* hath been the greatest engine of tyranny in the world."[26] He thus applauded the liberal and enlightened action of the delegates in prohibiting religious tests.

The third objection concerning religion was the most widespread: the lack of a Bill of Rights to safeguard freedom of religion. So prevalent was this concern that James Madison pledged to include amendments that would protect individual rights, including that of religion. He had initially opposed a Bill of Rights on the grounds that any enumeration of rights would be restrictive; that is, there could be those who argue that those rights, and only those rights, are protected. But, hearing protests from all the ratifying conventions and from such trusted friends as

---

[24] Elliott, ed., *The Debates in the Several State Conventions, on the Adoption of the Federal Constitution*, 2:44.

[25] Ibid., 4:199, 215.

[26] Ibid., 2:148.

Thomas Jefferson, he agreed to support the inclusion of a Bill of Rights. The result of his efforts to protect religious freedom was the first amendment that prohibited Congress from making any laws respecting the establishment of religion and that guaranteed the individual's right to the free exercise of religion.

In ignoring religion, the delegates were not indicating that they thought religion unimportant in the new republic. Quite to the contrary, most believed that religious instruction was key in the development of moral men and women and essential in creating a virtuous citizenry. But the importance of religion was not their central concern; rather, it was the *place* of religion in society. Should religion be state supported? If so, which religion? They knew that while most Americans were affiliated with Protestant churches, there were deeply held beliefs and practices that separated the various denominations. Therefore, any formulation, including that of simply "the Christian faith," was sure to raise fears and jealousies over issues of authority and control.

Many delegates took the position that religious questions had already been settled at the state level, and there they should stay. For the federal government to involve itself in religious matters was certain to strain the bonds of union rather than strengthening them. Thus, religion was seldom discussed at the convention.

In the case of religious matters, how did the delegates separate church and state under the Constitution? First, fearing any government encroachment on religion, they granted no power to Congress or the federal government regarding religion. Congress received extraordinary grants of power regarding taxation, war, peace, commerce, etc., but none involving religion. Consequently, there would be no national church or religion, like there was in most

European countries at the time. Second, fearing religious infringement on civil liberties, the delegates prohibited any religious tests for officeholders. One's religious beliefs and affiliations would have no bearing on his or her qualifications for holding office, including that of the Presidency.

The practical result of the constitutional separation of church and state was the creation of what Adam Smith described as "a free marketplace of religion." Writing in *The Wealth of Nations* (1776), Smith envisioned a free exchange of religious ideas just as he advocated free trade in goods. The key, he argued, was to remove all government monopolies and favors to an established religion. In a country with no establishment, there would be a multitude of sects freely promulgating their respective views. Faced with such competition, "each teacher would no doubt [feel] himself under the necessity of making the utmost exertion and of using every art both to preserve and to increase the number of his disciples." Not only would voluntary religion in a free market make religious leaders more industrious, it would check religious fanaticism. Smith argued that religious "zeal must be altogether innocent where the society is divided into two or three hundred, or perhaps into as many thousand small sects, of which no one could be considerable enough to disturb the public tranquility." He concluded that "if politics had never [been] called in the aid of religion," every person would "choose his own priest and his own religion as he thought proper."[27]

Near the end of his life, Madison reflected on how the nation had fared under the Constitution he had helped

---

[27] Adam Smith, *An Inquiry into the Nature and Causes of the Wealth of Nations*, 2 vols., ed. R.H. Campbell and A.S. Skinner (Indianapolis: Liberty Fund, 1981) 2:792–93.

craft. In particular he was pleased with the way religion had fared. By separating church and state, by making the support of religion voluntary, churches were numerous and vigorous. Allowed to pursue their respective faiths as they wished, American believers expressed their religious views with energy unheard of where an established church enjoyed state support. He noted that both church and state had flourished under the principle of separation and provided Americans today a clear answer to the question of the separation of church and state. He wrote, "The civil Government, though bereft of everything like an associated hierarchy, possesses the requisite stability, and performs its functions with complete success, whilst the number, the industry, and the morality of the priesthood, and the devotion of the people, have been manifestly increased by the total separation of the church from the State."[28] While Christian Right "historians" view the separation of church and state as a liberal myth, the principal architect of the Constitution saw it as a founding principle of religious liberty.

---

[28] Hunt, ed., *The Writings of Madison*, vol. 8, Letter to Robert Walsh, 2 March 1819.

Index

SEPARATION OF CHURCH AND STATE